MASTER DECIMALS

Math Practice Workbook with Answers

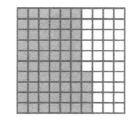

Chris McMullen, Ph.D.

Master Decimals Math Practice Workbook with Answers
Chris McMullen, Ph.D.

Copyright © 2020 Chris McMullen, Ph.D.

www.improveyourmathfluency.com
www.monkeyphysicsblog.wordpress.com
www.chrismcmullen.com

All rights are reserved. However, educators or parents who purchase one copy of this workbook (or who borrow one physical copy from a library) may make and distribute photocopies of selected pages for instructional (non-commercial) purposes for their own students or children only.

Zishka Publishing
ISBN: 978-1-941691-55-7

Mathematics > Arithmetic > Decimals
Study Guides > Workbooks > Math

CONTENTS

Introduction	iv
1 Decimal Place Values	5
2 Compare Decimals	19
3 Add and Subtract Decimals	29
4 Multiply Decimals	43
5 Divide Decimals	77
6 Fractions and Decimals	107
7 Repeating Decimals	123
8 Percents and Decimals	147
9 Estimate with Decimals	159
Answer Key	167

INTRODUCTION

The goal of this workbook is to help students master decimal skills through practice. A variety of essential skills are included, such as:
- understanding what a decimal is
- decimal place values
- visualizing decimals
- comparing decimals
- how to add or subtract decimals
- how to multiply or divide decimals
- visualizing calculations that involve decimals
- converting between fractions and decimals
- repeating decimals
- converting between percents and decimals
- rounding decimals
- estimating decimal calculations
- exponents of decimals
- square roots of decimals
- a variety of calculations involving decimals
- word problems with decimals

You can find the answers to all of the problems at the back of the book. Practice makes permanent, but not necessarily perfect. Check the answers at the back of the book and strive to learn from any mistakes. This will help to ensure that practice makes perfect.

1 DECIMAL PLACE VALUES

hundreds	tens	units	.	tenths	hundredths	thousandths
4	2	9	.	7	6	3

$$429.763 = 400 + 20 + 9 + \frac{7}{10} + \frac{6}{100} + \frac{3}{1000}$$

$$429.763 = 400 + 20 + 9 + 0.7 + 0.06 + 0.003$$

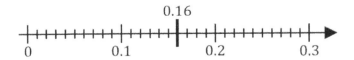

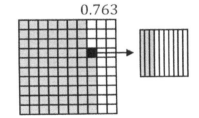

1 Decimal Place Values

1.1 What Is a Decimal?

A <u>decimal</u> is a fraction where the denominator is 10, 100, 1000, or a higher power of 10. The denominator is indicated by the position of a point called the <u>decimal point</u>. To determine the denominator of the equivalent fraction, count the number of digits to the right of the decimal point; this determines the number of zeros that follow 1 in the denominator. See the examples below.

Example 1. 0.3 has one decimal digit. It is equivalent to $\frac{3}{10}$.

Example 2. 0.49 has two decimal digits. It is equivalent to $\frac{49}{100}$.

Example 3. 0.638 has three decimal digits. It is equivalent to $\frac{638}{1000}$. (Note that $\frac{638}{1000}$ is a reducible fraction because 638 and 1000 are each evenly divisible by 2. You do not need to reduce fractions in this section. We will reduce fractions in Chapter 6.)

Example 4. 2.1 has one decimal digit. It is equivalent to $\frac{21}{10}$. (Note that $\frac{21}{10}$ is an improper fraction because the numerator is larger than the denominator. We could alternatively express it as $2\frac{1}{10}$, meaning two and one tenth. If the decimal number includes nonzero digits to the left of the decimal point, like the 2 in 2.1, the fraction will be improper. Even though we use the word "improper," such fractions are quite common. There is nothing wrong with expressing fractions in this form.)

Example 5. 0.007 has one decimal digit. It is equivalent to $\frac{7}{1000}$. (Note that the leading decimal zeros disappear in the numerator of the equivalent fraction: 007 makes 7 in the numerator. We will learn more about leading and trailing zeros in Sec. 2.1.)

Exercise Set 1.1

Directions: Express each decimal as an equivalent fraction.

1) 0.7 =

2) 0.61 =

3) 0.819 =

4) 0.5 =

5) 0.24 =

6) 0.017 =

7) 8.1 =

8) 0.376 =

9) 0.09 =

10) 15.2 =

11) 1.63 =

12) 0.0001 =

13) 0.543 =

14) 2.5 =

15) 0.36 =

16) 0.003 =

17) 17.54 =

18) 0.6 =

19) 1.001 =

20) 0.0505 =

1.2 Place Value Charts

Every digit in a number has a <u>**place value**</u>. For example, in the whole number 4317, the 4 is in the thousands place, the 3 is in the hundreds place, the 1 is in the tens place, and the 7 is in the <u>**units**</u> place. (The units place may alternatively be called the ones place.) When digits appear to the right of a decimal point, the place values are called tenths, hundredths, thousandths, and so on. For example, in the decimal 0.659, the 6 is in the tenths place, the 5 is in the hundredths place, and the 9 is in the thousandths place.

4	2	9	.	7	6	3
hundreds	tens	units		tenths	hundredths	thousandths

Two letters can make a huge difference. It pays to read carefully. For example, in the number 429.763, the 4 is in the hundreds place whereas the 6 is in the hundred<u>**ths**</u> place. Similarly, the 2 is in the tens place whereas the 7 is in the ten<u>**th**</u>s place.

An easy way to see the place value of each digit is to write the number in a <u>**place value chart**</u>. For example, the number 429.763 was written in a place value chart below by writing each digit in the appropriate column. The decimal point determines all of the place values. For example, the units digit appears just left of the decimal point, while the tenths digit appears just right of the decimal point.

hundreds	tens	units	.	tenths	hundredths	thousandths
4	2	9	.	7	6	3

Example 1. Write the number 7215.48 in the place value chart below.
The digits 7215 appear to the left of the decimal point, while the digits 48 appear to the right of the decimal point.

thousands	hundreds	tens	units	.	tenths	hundredths
7	2	1	5	.	4	8

Exercise Set 1.2

Directions: Write each number in the place value chart.

1) 3.5 =

thousands	hundreds	tens	units	.	tenths	hundredths	thousandths
				.			

2) 6.792 =

thousands	hundreds	tens	units	.	tenths	hundredths	thousandths
				.			

3) 42.15 =

thousands	hundreds	tens	units	.	tenths	hundredths	thousandths
				.			

4) 0.089 =

thousands	hundreds	tens	units	.	tenths	hundredths	thousandths
				.			

5) 653.02 =

thousands	hundreds	tens	units	.	tenths	hundredths	thousandths
				.			

6) 4.634 =

thousands	hundreds	tens	units	.	tenths	hundredths	thousandths
				.			

7) 5726.3 =

thousands	hundreds	tens	units	.	tenths	hundredths	thousandths
				.			

8) 2415.987 =

thousands	hundreds	tens	units	.	tenths	hundredths	thousandths
				.			

1.3 Expanded Form (Using Fractions)

Another way to show the place value of each digit in a number is to write the number in expanded form. For example, the expanded form of a whole number adds together the units, tens, hundreds, thousands, etc. For example, when the whole number 728 is written in expanded form, it is $700 + 20 + 8$. The same idea applies to decimals. We can express the tenths digit as a fraction with a denominator of 10, the hundredths digit as a fraction with a denominator of 100, etc. For example, when the number 0.83 is written in expanded form, it is $\frac{8}{10} + \frac{3}{100}$.

Example 1. $4.7 = 4 + \frac{7}{10}$

Example 2. $0.561 = \frac{5}{10} + \frac{6}{100} + \frac{1}{1000}$

Example 3. $524.08 = 500 + 20 + 4 + \frac{0}{10} + \frac{8}{100}$ which simplifies to $500 + 20 + 4 + \frac{8}{100}$

Exercise Set 1.3

Directions: Write each number in expanded form (using fractions for decimals).

1) $65.2 =$

2) $1.49 =$

3) $0.0083 =$

4) $729.165 =$

5) $0.4803 =$

6) $9047.1032 =$

1.4 Expanded Form (Using Decimals)

There are two ways to write a number in expanded form:
- One way is to use fractions, like $58.34 = 50 + 8 + \frac{3}{10} + \frac{4}{100}$.
- Another way is to use decimals, like $58.34 = 50 + 8 + 0.3 + 0.04$.

In this section, we will expand numbers using the decimal form.

Example 1. $87.34 = 80 + 7 + 0.3 + 0.04$
Example 2. $0.125 = 0.1 + 0.02 + 0.005$
Example 3. $209.1 = 200 + 0 + 9 + 0.1$ which simplifies to $200 + 9 + 0.1$

Exercise Set 1.4

Directions: Write each number in expanded form (using decimals).

1) $4.63 =$

2) $38.2 =$

3) $4.657 =$

4) $8256.4 =$

5) $0.00971 =$

6) $42.105 =$

7) $70.4902 =$

8) $808.0303 =$

1.5 Word Form of Decimals

To write a decimal number in word form, follow these steps:
- For the digits to the left of the decimal point, write the word form as you would normally write the word form for a whole number. For example, the digits to the left of the decimal point in 362.749 are 362, which are "three hundred sixty-two" in word form. (Note that the word "and" is not used after the hundred.)
- Write the word "and" for the decimal point. (We will only use the word "and" for the decimal point.)
- For the digits to the right of the decimal point, first write the word form as you would normally write the word form for a whole number. Then add the word for the place value of the final digit. (It may help to review the place value charts in Sec. 1.2.) Include the letter "s" at the end of this word (unless the only nonzero digit is a one; see the note to the solution to Problem 9). For example, the digits to the right of the decimal point in 362.749 are 749, which are "seven hundred forty-nine" in word form. The final digit, which is a 9, is in the thousandths place. The word form of 362.749 is:

362.749 = three hundred sixty-two and seven hundred forty-nine thousandths

Example 1. 26.53 = twenty-six and fifty-three hundredths
Example 2. 418.266 = four hundred eighteen and two hundred sixty-six thousandths
Example 3. 8.0023 = eight and twenty-three ten thousandths (Note that the 3 is in the ten thousandths place. The next place value is the hundred thousandths, after that is the millionths, etc.)

Exercise Set 1.5

Directions: Write each decimal in word form.

1) 4.7 =

Master Decimals Math Practice Workbook with Answers

2) 31.85 =

3) 76.573 =

4) 390.19 =

5) 7.07 =

6) 456,192.8 =

7) 0.0027 =

8) 84.716 =

9) 0.000001 =

10) 3.08621 =

1.6 Place Values

As we saw in Sec. 1.2, the position of the decimal point determines the place value of each digit in a number. For example, consider the number 384.27695:
- the 3 is in the hundreds place
- the 8 is in the tens place
- the 4 is in the units place (also called the ones place)
- the 2 is in the tenths place
- the 7 is in the hundredths place
- the 6 is in the thousandths place
- the 9 is in the ten thousandths place
- the 5 is in the hundred thousandths place

Place values to the left of the decimal point do not have a "th," whereas place values to the right of the decimal point do have a "th." For example, compare the 8 in the tens place to the 2 in the tenths place.

Example 1. In 7.043, the 4 is in the hundredths place.
Example 2. In 0.0589, the 8 is in the thousandths place.
Example 3. In 47.1, the 1 is in the tenths place.
Example 4. In 0.0036, the 6 is in the ten thousandths place.

Exercise Set 1.6

Directions: Name the place value of the indicated digit.

1) the 6 in 2.016

2) the 5 in 35.12

3) the 2 in 0.527

4) the 4 in 6.48

5) the 9 in 94.73

6) the 1 in 0.015

7) the 8 in 384.6

8) the 3 in 4.023

9) the 0 in 16.09

10) the 7 in 27,456.8

11) the 4 in 0.03742

12) the 6 in 54,328.961

13) the 9 in 6.304189

14) the 1 in 0.00146

15) the 5 in 3.28375

1.7 Base-10 Blocks

One way to draw a picture of a decimal is to use **base-10 blocks**. These are building blocks based on the following powers of ten: 1, 0.1, 0.01, and 0.001.

- One full square represents 1 square unit. This is called the **unit square**.
- If the unit square is divided into 10 strips, each strip has a value of 0.1 (a tenth).
- If the unit square is divided into a 10 × 10 grid, the grid has 100 tiny squares. Each tiny square has a value of 0.01 (a hundredth). The 10 × 10 grid is called the **decimal square**. (This square is convenient for drawing decimals.)
- To draw thousandths, one tiny square from the 10 × 10 grid can be magnified and divided into 10 tiny strips. Each tiny strip has a value of 0.001 (a thousandth).

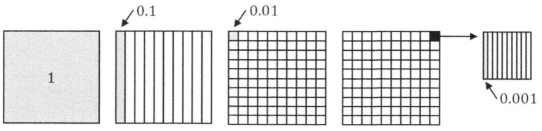

Example 1. Draw a picture to represent 0.8.
Divide the unit square into 10 strips. Shade 8 of the strips gray.

Example 2. Draw a picture to represent 0.47.
Divide the unit square into a 10 × 10 grid. Shade 4 columns gray plus 7 tiny squares of another column.

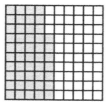

Example 3. Draw a picture to represent 0.763.

Divide the unit square into a 10 × 10 grid. Shade 7 columns gray plus 6 tiny squares of another column plus 3 tiny strips of a magnified tiny square.

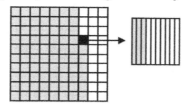

Exercise Set 1.7

Directions: Draw the decimal by shading squares.

1) 0.3 =

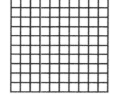

2) 0.73 =

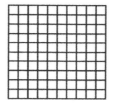

3) 0.487 =

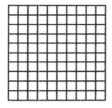

4) 0.9 =

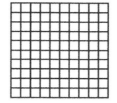

5) 0.25 =

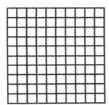

6) 0.068 =

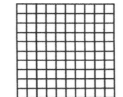

1.8 Decimals on a Number Line

Another way to picture a decimal is to draw it on a number line with evenly spaced tick marks. For example, the number line below has small tick marks and large tick marks. The large tick marks are labeled 0, 1, 2, and 3. The small tick marks in between are 0.1, 0.2, 0.3, etc. After reaching 1, they are 1.1, 1.2, 1.3, etc. After reaching 2, they are 2.1, 2.2, 2.3, etc. The decimal 1.6 is drawn as an example.

Example 1. Draw and label 0.42 on the number line below.

This number line has large tick marks of 0.1, 0.2, 0.3, 0.4, 0.5 and small tick marks of 0.01, 0.02, 0.03, etc., which is different from the number line shown above.

Exercise Set 1.8

Directions: Draw and label all of the given values on the number line.

1) 0.3, 1.1, 1.5, 2.2

2) 0.07, 0.25, 0.32, 0.46

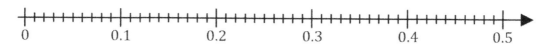

3) 0.004, 0.019, 0.021, 0.028

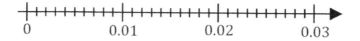

2 COMPARE DECIMALS

$$0.354 < 0.355$$

$$0.1 > 0.09$$

$$0.5 = 0.500$$

$$1, 0.7, 0.08, 0.9 \rightarrow 0.08 < 0.7 < 0.9 < 1$$

$$0.46, 0.45, 0.448, 0.453 \rightarrow 0.448 < 0.45 < 0.453 < 0.46$$

$$0.021, 0.019, 0.004, 0.028 \rightarrow 0.004 < 0.019 < 0.021 < 0.028$$

2.1 Leading and Trailing Zeros

Zeros that appear at the beginning of a number are called **leading zeros**, whereas zeros that appear at the end of a number are called **trailing zeros**. For example:
- 0.0025 has three leading zeros. Two of these are decimal leading zeros.
- 1.500 has two trailing zeros. All of these are decimal trailing zeros.
- 450 has one trailing zero. It is not a decimal trailing zero.
- 70.0 has two trailing zeros. One of these is a decimal trailing zero.
- 0.0180000 has two leading zeros and four trailing zeros. One of the leading zeros is a decimal leading zero, and it ends with four decimal trailing zeros.

When a decimal number is smaller than one, like 0.8, 0.07, or 0.0032, we often write a leading zero before the decimal point. A leading zero that appears to the left of the decimal point is optional (like 0.6, which equals .6). Leading zeros that appear to the right of the decimal point matter. For example:
- 0.8 is equivalent to .8
- 0.07 is equivalent to .07
- 0.0032 is equivalent to .0032

Trailing zeros that are decimals are optional. For example:
- 6.20 is equivalent to 6.2
- 0.4500 is equivalent to 0.45
- 0.0071000 is equivalent to 0.0071
- 120.0 is equivalent to 120
- The zeros in 2400 matter because they do not appear to the right of a decimal point.

Example 1. 3.800 has two trailing zeros and is equivalent to 3.8
Example 2. 0.05 has two leading zeros and is equivalent to .05
Example 3. 40.000 has four trailing zeros and is equivalent to 40
Example 4. 0.00160000 has three leading zeros and four trailing zeros; it is equivalent to 0.0016 and .0016

Exercise Set 2.1

Directions: For each number, indicate how many leading zeros and how many trailing zeros there are. Also, if any of the leading zeros or trailing zeros may be removed from the number, rewrite the number in an equivalent form without those zeros.

1) 0.6

2) 7.200

3) 0.008

4) 20.00

5) 0.010

6) 600,010.0

7) 5.00000

8) 0.0037600

9) 0.04440000

10) 40,000.0

2.2 Check One Decimal Place

To compare two decimal numbers, identify the leading nonzero digit of each number. This is the first nonzero digit at the left of the number.

- If either leading nonzero digit has a greater place value, that number is larger. In this case, it does not matter which digit is larger. For example, compare 0.2 with 0.08. The leading nonzero digit of 0.2 is the 2, which is in the tenths place. The leading nonzero digit of 0.08 is the 8, which is in the hundredths place. Since a tenth is greater than a hundredth, 0.2 is greater than 0.08.
- If the leading nonzero digits have the same place value, if the leading nonzero digits are different, the number with the greater leading nonzero digit is larger. For example, compare 0.07 to 0.03. The leading nonzero digit of each number is in the hundredths place. Therefore, 0.07 is greater than 0.03 because 7 is greater than 3.
- If the leading nonzero digits have the same place value and are the same digit, like 0.54 and 0.56, we need to look at the next digit (Sec.'s 2.3-2.5).

The **greater than** symbol (>) indicates that the left value is larger than the right value. For example, 0.9 > 0.4. The **less than** symbol (<) indicates that the left value is smaller than the right value. For example, 0.02 < 0.05. Note that in both cases the vertex of the > or < symbol points toward the smaller value.

Example 1. Compare 0.007 to 0.0062.
In each case, the leading nonzero digit is in the thousandths place. Since the leading nonzero digits have the same place value, the number with the greater leading nonzero digit is greater. This means that 0.007 is greater than 0.0062. Since 0.007 is on the left, use the greater than symbol: 0.007 > 0.0062.

Example 2. Compare 0.004 to 0.03.
The leading nonzero digit of 0.004 is in the thousandths place and the leading nonzero digit of 0.03 is in the hundredths place. Since a hundredth is larger than a thousandth, 0.03 is greater than 0.004 (which means that 0.004 is less than 0.03). Since 0.004 is on the left, use the less than symbol: 0.004 < 0.03.

Exercise Set 2.2

Directions: Write <, >, or = between each pair of numbers.

1) 0.5   0.6

2) 0.3   0.04

3) 0.2   0.20

4) 0.08   0.07

5) 0.08   0.009

6) 0.6   0.7

7) 0.9   1

8) 0.0300   0.030

9) 0.004   0.003

10) 0.0005   0.004

11) 4.2   3.7

12) 0.58   0.7

13) 0.27   0.072

14) 0.081   0.018

15) 0.6   0.094

16) 0.0029   0.0031

17) 0.055   0.06

18) 2.1   1.975

19) 0.088   0.09

20) 0.0999   0.1

2.3 Check Two Decimal Places

If the leading nonzero digits have the same place value and are the same digit, like 0.54 and 0.56, the next digit determines which number is greater. In the case of 0.54 and 0.56, the leading nonzero digit is 5 in each case. Since 4 is less than 6, it follows that $0.54 < 0.56$. If the second digits are the same, like 0.473 and 0.474, we need to look at the third digit (Sec. 2.4).

Example 1. Compare 0.063 to 0.064.
In each case, the leading nonzero digit is a 6 in the hundredths place. Since the leading nonzero digit has the same place value and is the same digit, look at the next digit. Since 3 is less than 4, it follows that $0.063 < 0.064$.

Exercise Set 2.3

Directions: Write $<$, $>$, or $=$ between each pair of numbers.

1) 0.85   0.87   2) 0.033   0.032

3) 2.6   2.5   4) 0.0098   0.0099

5) 0.073   0.07   6) 0.4   0.40

7) 0.5   0.058   8) 0.006   0.0061

9) 0.127   0.14   10) 0.0027   0.00028

11) 8.3   8   12) 0.0911   0.09

2.4 Check Three Decimal Places

If the leading nonzero digits have the same place value and are the same digit, and the same is true of the next digit, like 0.317 and 0.315, the following digit determines which number is greater. For 0.317 and 0.315, the leading nonzero digit is 3 in each case and the next digit is 1 in each case. The following digit determines that 0.317 is greater than 0.315 (since 0.31 is the same for each and $7 > 5$).

Example 1. Compare 0.728 to 0.725.
Since 0.72 is the same for each and $8 > 5$, it follows that $0.728 > 0.725$.

Exercise Set 2.4

Directions: Write $<$, $>$, or $=$ between each pair of numbers.

1) 0.493   0.494

2) 2.36   2.354

3) 0.0555   0.055

4) 0.77   0.770

5) 0.02478   0.247

6) 61.4   61

7) 1.787   1.792

8) 0.924   0.942

9) 0.1001   0.101

10) 0.04000   0.04

11) 6.012   6

12) 0.0303   0.03003

2.5 Compare Decimals

The exercises in this section are a mix of ideas from Sec.'s 2.1-2.4.

Exercise Set 2.5

Directions: Write <, >, or = between each pair of numbers.

1) 0.5   0.05

2) 0.35   0.57

3) 0.009   0.0009

4) 2.65   2.6

5) 0.0456   0.053

6) 0.02   0.1

7) 1.1   0.7

8) 0.269   0.268

9) 0.0434   0.434

10) 0.01   0.010

11) 0.22   0.202

12) 0.47   0.5

13) 8.546   8.564

14) 0.0971   0.09712

15) 0.67337   0.6734

16) 8.25149   8.2515

17) 0.000067   0.00021

18) 9.0999   9.1

2.6 Order Three Decimals

To put three decimal numbers in order, compare them to determine which is the least and which is the greatest.

Example 1. Order 0.37, 0.03, and 0.4 from least to greatest.
Note that 0.37 > 0.03 because tenths > hundredths, 0.37 < 0.4 because 0.3 < 0.4, and 0.03 < 0.4 because hundredths < tenths. The least value is 0.03 (because it is smaller than 0.37 and 0.4). The greatest value is 0.4 (because it is greater than 0.37 and 0.03). In order from least to greatest, these numbers are: 0.03, 0.37, and 0.4.

Exercise Set 2.6

Directions: Rewrite each list of numbers in order from least to greatest.

1) 0.6, 0.4, 0.5

2) 0.003, 0.1, 0.02

3) 0.59, 0.61, 0.6

4) 0.075, 0.07, 0.08

5) 0.442, 0.444, 0.44

6) 2.35, 2.34, 2.43

7) 0.7071, 0.707, 0.71

8) 0.000289, 0.00029, 0.0017

9) 50, 49.9, 50.5

10) 0.091, 0.09, 0.1

2.7 Order Four Decimals

The exercises in this section have four decimal numbers in each list.

Example 1. Order 0.6, 0.058, 0.4, and 0.052 from least to greatest.
Of these, the smallest number is 0.052 and the largest number is 0.6. Of the numbers in between, $0.058 < 0.4$ because hundredths are smaller than tenths. In order from least to greatest, these numbers are: $0.052 < 0.058 < 0.4 < 0.6$.

Exercise Set 2.7

Directions: Rewrite each list of numbers in order from least to greatest.

1) 0.5, 0.05, 0.065, 0.06

2) 1.11, 1.1, 1.212, 1.2

3) 0.1, 0.03, 0.007, 0.009

4) 0.01, 0.2, 0.025, 0.006

5) 4.24, 4.238, 4.242, 4.097

6) 0.01, 0.001, 0.015, 0.0015

7) 0.6432, 0.4632, 0.6342, 0.6324

8) 1.00062, 1.0054, 1.048, 1.1

9) 0.07, 0.08, 0.0078, 0.0087

10) 0.5, 0.49, 0.501, 0.499

11) 2, 2.1, 2.09, 1.999

12) 6.543, 6.54211, 6.54223, 6.54201

3 ADD AND SUBTRACT DECIMALS

$$\begin{array}{r} {}^{1} \\ 2.7 \\ +\ 1.8 \\ \hline 4.5 \end{array}$$

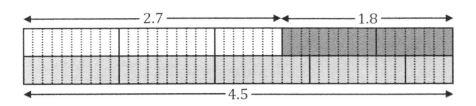

$$\begin{array}{r} {}^{1}\,{}^{13} \\ 2.\cancel{3} \\ -\ 1.4 \\ \hline 0.9 \end{array}$$

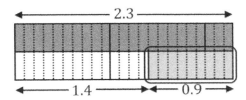

3 Add and Subtract Decimals

3.1 Add One-Digit Decimals

Adding decimals is similar to adding whole numbers, with a few differences:
- Write one number above the other. Line the numbers up at their decimal points.
- If one number has fewer decimal places than the other number (like $0.8 + 0.07$), add trailing zeros until both numbers have the same final decimal position. For $0.8 + 0.07$, rewrite 0.8 as 0.80. Now the problem is $0.80 + 0.07$.
- Add the numbers like you would normally add whole numbers, but include a decimal point in the same position as the numbers that you added.

$$\begin{array}{r} 0.80 \\ + 0.07 \\ \hline 0.87 \end{array}$$

Example 1. What is $0.8 + 0.4$?

Stack the numbers one above the other. Line them up at their decimal points.

$$\begin{array}{r} 0.8 \\ + 0.4 \\ \hline 1.2 \end{array}$$

Example 2. What is $0.8 + 0.04$?

Stack the numbers one above the other. Line them up at their decimal points. Since 0.8 ends in the tenths and 0.04 ends in the hundredths, add a trailing zero to make 0.80.

$$\begin{array}{r} 0.80 \\ + 0.04 \\ \hline 0.84 \end{array}$$

Example 3. What is $0.08 + 0.4$?

Stack the numbers one above the other. Line them up at their decimal points. Since 0.08 ends in the hundredths and 0.4 ends in the tenths, add a trailing zero to make 0.40.

$$\begin{array}{r} 0.08 \\ + 0.40 \\ \hline 0.48 \end{array}$$

Example 4. What is $0.08 + 0.04$?

Stack the numbers one above the other. Line them up at their decimal points.

$$\begin{array}{r} 0.08 \\ + 0.04 \\ \hline 0.12 \end{array}$$

Exercise Set 3.1

9/22/2023

Directions: Add the numbers.

1)
$$\begin{array}{r} 0.4 \\ +\ 0.2 \\ \hline 0.6 \end{array}$$

2)
$$\begin{array}{r} 0.7 \\ +\ 0.6 \\ \hline 1.3 \end{array}$$

3)
$$\begin{array}{r} 0.09 \\ +\ 0.10 \\ \hline 0.19 \end{array}$$

4)
$$\begin{array}{r} 0.08 \\ +\ 0.07 \\ \hline 0.15 \end{array}$$

5)
$$\begin{array}{r} 0.3 \\ +\ 0.06 \\ \hline 0.36 \end{array}$$

6)
$$\begin{array}{r} 0.008 \\ +\ 0.005 \\ \hline 0.013 \end{array}$$

7)
$$\begin{array}{r} 0.6 \\ +\ 0.4 \\ \hline 1.0 \end{array}$$

8)
$$\begin{array}{r} 0.09 \\ +\ 0.09 \\ \hline 0.19 \end{array}$$

9)
$$\begin{array}{r} 2 \\ +\ 0.8 \\ \hline 2.8 \end{array}$$

10)
$$\begin{array}{r} 0.4 \\ +\ 0.04 \\ \hline \end{array}$$

11)
$$\begin{array}{r} 0.07 \\ +\ 0.05 \\ \hline \end{array}$$

12)
$$\begin{array}{r} 0.009 \\ +\ 0.06 \\ \hline \end{array}$$

13) $0.8 + 0.6 =$

14) $0.7 + 0.04 =$

15) $0.05 + 0.05 =$

16) $0.06 + 0.2 =$

17) $0.09 + 0.08 =$

18) $1 + 0.4 =$

3.2 Subtract One-Digit Decimals

Subtracting decimals is similar to subtracting whole numbers, with a few differences:
- Write one number above the other. Line the numbers up at their decimal points.
- If one number has fewer decimal places than the other number (like $0.1 - 0.03$), add trailing zeros until both numbers have the same final decimal position. For $0.1 - 0.03$, rewrite 0.1 as 0.10. Now the problem is $0.10 - 0.03$.
- Subtract the numbers like you would normally subtract whole numbers, but include a decimal point in the same position as the subtracted numbers.
- As with ordinary subtraction, it may be necessary to regroup (or borrow). For example, with $0.10 - 0.03$ (see below), the 1 may be regrouped with the 0 to make 10. Also see Example 2.

$$\begin{array}{r} {\scriptstyle 0\ 10} \\ 0.\cancel{1}\cancel{0} \\ -\ 0.03 \\ \hline 0.07 \end{array}$$

Example 1. What is $0.7 - 0.2$?

Stack the numbers one above the other. Line them up at their decimal points.

$$\begin{array}{r} 0.7 \\ -\ 0.2 \\ \hline 0.5 \end{array}$$

Example 2. What is $0.7 - 0.02$?

Stack the numbers one above the other. Line them up at their decimal points. Since 0.7 ends in the tenths and 0.02 ends in the hundredths, add a trailing zero to make 0.70. Regroup (or borrow): Reduce the 7 to a 6 to turn the 0 into a 10.

$$\begin{array}{r} {\scriptstyle 6\ 10} \\ 0.\cancel{7}\cancel{0} \\ -\ 0.02 \\ \hline 0.68 \end{array}$$

Example 3. What is $0.07 - 0.02$?

Stack the numbers one above the other. Line them up at their decimal points.

$$\begin{array}{r} 0.07 \\ -\ 0.02 \\ \hline 0.05 \end{array}$$

Exercise Set 3.2

Directions: Subtract the numbers.

1)
$$\begin{array}{r} 0.9 \\ -0.3 \\ \hline \end{array}$$

2)
$$\begin{array}{r} 1.2 \\ -0.5 \\ \hline \end{array}$$

3)
$$\begin{array}{r} 0.1 \\ -0.04 \\ \hline \end{array}$$

4)
$$\begin{array}{r} 0.08 \\ -0.06 \\ \hline \end{array}$$

5)
$$\begin{array}{r} 0.15 \\ -0.07 \\ \hline \end{array}$$

6)
$$\begin{array}{r} 0.2 \\ -0.09 \\ \hline \end{array}$$

7)
$$\begin{array}{r} 0.83 \\ -0.2 \\ \hline \end{array}$$

8)
$$\begin{array}{r} 0.007 \\ -0.003 \\ \hline \end{array}$$

9)
$$\begin{array}{r} 1.4 \\ -0.7 \\ \hline \end{array}$$

10)
$$\begin{array}{r} 1 \\ -0.5 \\ \hline \end{array}$$

11)
$$\begin{array}{r} 0.012 \\ -0.004 \\ \hline \end{array}$$

12)
$$\begin{array}{r} 0.1 \\ -0.01 \\ \hline \end{array}$$

13) $0.8 - 0.4 =$

14) $0.63 - 0.3 =$

15) $1.1 - 0.5 =$

16) $0.6 - 0.04 =$

17) $1.7 - 0.7 =$

18) $0.04 - 0.003 =$

3.3 Add Decimals with Strip Diagrams

One way to draw pictures of decimal addition is to make strip diagrams. For decimals with units and tenths (like 2.7 + 1.8), follow these steps to draw a strip diagram:

- Draw a single rectangular strip to represent one unit. Divide the unit strip into 10 smaller pieces. Each small piece represents one tenth (0.1).
- Draw unit strips and small pieces to make the first decimal. For example, to draw 2.7, draw 2 unit strips and 7 small pieces. To draw the 7 small pieces, imagine drawing one strip, dividing the strip into 10 equal pieces, and removing 3 of the small pieces. The small pieces need to all be the same length.
- Draw unit strips and small pieces to make the second decimal. Draw these next to the first decimal so that the strips and small pieces are added together. For example, to draw 1.8, draw 1 unit strip and 8 small pieces. To draw the 8 small pieces, imagine drawing one strip, dividing the strip into 10 equal pieces, and removing 2 of the small pieces. The small pieces need to all be the same length.
- Under the strips that have already been drawn, first draw as many unit strips as you can without exceeding the length of the strips that were already drawn. Divide each unit strip into 10 equal pieces. The small pieces on the bottom need to match the small pieces on the top. After drawing as many unit strips as you can, draw small pieces until all of the strips on the top and the bottom have the same combined length. See the example below.
- Count the unit strips and small pieces on the bottom. This is the answer. In the example below, 2.7 + 1.8 = 4.5 because the bottom row has 4 unit strips and 5 small pieces. Recall that each small piece is one-tenth (0.1).

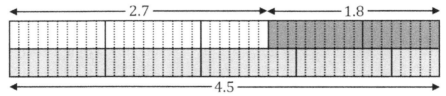

In the strip diagram above, we drew 2.7 as 2 unit strips plus 7 small pieces. Then we drew 1.8 as 1 unit strip plus 8 small pieces. Below these, we drew 4 unit strips and 5 small pieces. This shows visually that 2.7 plus 1.8 is equal to 4.5.

Example 1. Draw a strip diagram for 1.5 + 0.7.

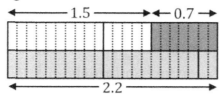

This strip diagram shows visually that 1.5 + 0.7 = 2.2.

Exercise Set 3.3

Directions: Draw a strip diagram to add the numbers.

1) 0.8 + 0.7

2) 2.4 + 1.6

3) 1.9 + 1.4

3.4 Subtract Decimals with Strip Diagrams

Drawing strip diagrams for subtraction is very similar to drawing strip diagrams for addition. Here is what is different for subtraction:
- Draw strips for the first number on the top row by itself.
- Draw strips for the second number below it, starting at the left.
- Now join strips to the second row until the two rows have the same combined length. The strips added to the second row form the answer. The strip diagram below shows $2.3 - 1.4 = 0.9$. The answer (0.9) is circled.

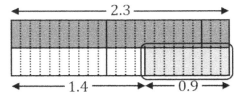

Example 1. Draw a strip diagram for $3.2 - 0.8$.

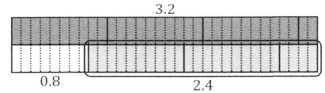

This strip diagram shows visually that $3.2 - 0.8 = 2.4$.

Exercise Set 3.4

Directions: Draw a strip diagram to subtract the numbers.

1) $2 - 1.3$ 2) $2.5 - 0.7$

3.5 Add Multi-Digit Decimals

Multi-digit decimals can be added using the strategy from Sec. 3.1. As with ordinary addition, it may be necessary to regroup (or carry over), as shown in Example 1.

Example 1. What is $0.34 + 0.082$?
Stack the numbers one above the other. Line them up at their decimal points. Since 0.34 ends in the hundredths and 0.082 ends in the thousandths, add a trailing zero to make 0.340. Regroup (or carry over): write the 1 from $4 + 8 = 12$ above the 3.

$$\begin{array}{r} \overset{1}{}0.340 \\ +\,0.082 \\ \hline 0.422 \end{array}$$

Exercise Set 3.5

Directions: Add the numbers.

1)
$$\begin{array}{r} 4.5 \\ +\,2.3 \\ \hline \end{array}$$

2)
$$\begin{array}{r} 0.7 \\ +\,0.58 \\ \hline \end{array}$$

3)
$$\begin{array}{r} 0.851 \\ +\,0.463 \\ \hline \end{array}$$

4)
$$\begin{array}{r} 2.6 \\ +\,0.35 \\ \hline \end{array}$$

5)
$$\begin{array}{r} 2.74 \\ +\,0.9 \\ \hline \end{array}$$

6)
$$\begin{array}{r} 0.579 \\ +\,0.041 \\ \hline \end{array}$$

7)
$$\begin{array}{r} 0.61 \\ +\,0.3 \\ \hline \end{array}$$

8)
$$\begin{array}{r} 6 \\ +\,1.5 \\ \hline \end{array}$$

9)
$$\begin{array}{r} 2.4 \\ +\,0.6 \\ \hline \end{array}$$

10)
$$\begin{array}{r} 0.089 \\ +\,0.05 \\ \hline \end{array}$$

11)
$$\begin{array}{r} 39.7 \\ +\,18.4 \\ \hline \end{array}$$

12)
$$\begin{array}{r} 9.9 \\ +\,0.101 \\ \hline \end{array}$$

3 Add and Subtract Decimals

13) 0.56 + 0.39 =

14) 0.63 + 0.3 =

15) 5.82 + 0.25 =

16) 6.8 + 0.73 =

17) 0.08 + 0.057 =

18) 28.7 + 8.4 =

19) 0.47 + 0.082 =

20) 73.5 + 0.5 =

21) 0.404 + 0.0202 =

22) 7.36 + 5.81 =

23) 1.49 + 0.378 =

24) 0.078 + 0.032 =

25) 99.88 + 1.111 =

26) 0.634 + 0.189 =

27) 14.99 + 0.2 =

3.6 Subtract Multi-Digit Decimals

9/24/2023: # 1-6

Multi-digit decimals can be subtracted using the strategy from Sec. 3.2.

Example 1. What is $0.62 - 0.034$?

Stack the numbers one above the other. Line them up at their decimal points. Since 0.62 ends in the hundredths and 0.034 ends in the thousandths, add a trailing zero to make 0.620. Regroup (or borrow): Reduce the 2 to a 1 to turn the 0 into a 10 and reduce the 6 to a 5 to turn the 1 into an 11.

$$\begin{array}{r} {}^{5\ 11\ 10}\\ 0.6\cancel{2}0 \\ -\ 0.034 \\ \hline 0.586 \end{array}$$

Exercise Set 3.6

Directions: Subtract the numbers.

1)
$$\begin{array}{r} {}^{6}\\ 0.\cancel{7}2 \\ -\ 0.24 \\ \hline 0.48 \end{array}$$

2)
$$\begin{array}{r} {}^{7}\\ 8.\cancel{4}6 \\ -\ 0.9 \\ \hline 7.50 \end{array}$$

3)
$$\begin{array}{r} {}^{5}\\ 0.0\cancel{6}0 \\ -\ 0.015 \\ \hline 0.045 \end{array}$$

4)
$$\begin{array}{r} {}^{6}\\ 0.\cancel{7}16 \\ -\ 0.542 \\ \hline 0.174 \end{array}$$

5)
$$\begin{array}{r} {}^{6}\\ 0.0\cancel{7}3 \\ -\ 0.046 \\ \hline 0.027 \end{array}$$

6)
$$\begin{array}{r} {}^{5}\\ 0.3\cancel{6}1 \\ -\ 0.222 \\ \hline 0.139 \end{array}$$

7)
$$\begin{array}{r} 6.43 \\ -\ 3.59 \\ \hline \end{array}$$

8)
$$\begin{array}{r} 0.0096 \\ -\ 0.006 \\ \hline \end{array}$$

9/28

9)
$$\begin{array}{r} 63.5 \\ -\ 27.2 \\ \hline \end{array}$$

10)
$$\begin{array}{r} 4.236 \\ -\ 1.536 \\ \hline \end{array}$$

11)
$$\begin{array}{r} 1.256 \\ -\ 0.843 \\ \hline \end{array}$$

12)
$$\begin{array}{r} 8 \\ -\ 0.125 \\ \hline \end{array}$$

3 Add and Subtract Decimals

13) $5.6 - 4.9 =$

14) $0.7 - 0.23 =$

15) $1.41 - 0.41 =$

16) $0.736 - 0.285 =$

17) $13.8 - 5.3 =$

18) $0.097 - 0.08 =$

19) $0.6 - 0.25 =$

20) $8.45 - 3.7 =$

21) $0.581 - 0.492 =$

22) $2 - 0.79 =$

23) $0.926 - 0.543 =$

24) $0.038 - 0.0067 =$

25) $0.449 - 0.32 =$

26) $0.11 - 0.027 =$

27) $1.863 - 0.985 =$

3.7 Addition and Subtraction Word Problems

The word problems in this section involve adding or subtracting decimals.

Example 1. A set of colored pencils costs $4.80. The sales tax is $0.37. What is the total cost of the set of pencils?

Add the price of the set of pencils to the sales tax:

$$\begin{array}{r} \$4.80 \\ + \$0.37 \\ \hline \$5.17 \end{array}$$

Example 2. A rope is 3.5 feet long. The rope is cut into two pieces. One piece is 1.8 feet long. How long is the other piece?

Subtract the length of the first piece from the original length of the rope:

$$\begin{array}{r} 3.5 \\ - 1.8 \\ \hline 1.7 \end{array}$$

Exercise Set 3.7

Directions: Determine the answer to each word problem.

1) The length of a room is 10.25 feet. The width of the room is 2.75 feet shorter than the length of the room. How wide is the room?

2) A family hiked 2.8 miles along one trail and then hiked 1.5 miles along another trail. What total distance did the family travel?

3 Add and Subtract Decimals

3) Sam finished the race in 9.03 seconds. Pat finished the race 0.26 seconds earlier than Sam. How long did it take Pat to run the race?

4) During lunch, a student buys a sandwich that costs $1.75, a salad that costs $1.50, and a bottle of water that costs $0.85. (There is no sales tax.) What is the total cost of the student's lunch?

5) A rope is 5 feet long. The rope is cut into three pieces. One piece is 1.6 feet long and another piece is 2.7 feet long. How long is the remaining piece?

6) When a boy attempts to weigh a ball, the ball rolls off the scale. When the boy puts the ball in a small box and weighs the box and ball together, the scale reads 17.2 ounces. When the boy weighs the empty box, the scale reads 4.9 ounces. How much does the ball weigh?

7) At a movie theater, a medium popcorn costs $1.85 more than a small popcorn, and a large popcorn costs $1.55 more than a medium popcorn. What is the difference in price between a large popcorn and a small popcorn?

4 MULTIPLY DECIMALS

$$\begin{array}{r} \overset{3\ 2}{6.43} \\ \times\ 7 \\ \hline 45.01 \end{array}$$

$7 \times 6.43 = 7 \times 6 + 7 \times 0.4 + 7 \times 0.03$
$= 42 + 2.8 + 0.21 = 44.8 + 0.21 = 45.01$

$0.7 \times 0.5 = 0.35$

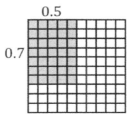

$1.4 \times 2.6 = 3.64$

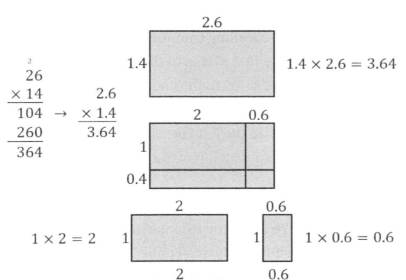

$1 \times 2 = 2$ $1 \times 0.6 = 0.6$

$0.4 \times 2 = 0.8$ $0.4 \times 0.6 = 0.24$

$2 + 0.6 + 0.8 + 0.24 = 3.64$

4 Multiply Decimals

4.1 Multiply Decimals by Powers of Ten

<u>Powers of ten</u> include 1, 10, 100, 1000, etc. and also include 0.1, 0.01, 0.001, 0.0001, etc. These numbers include a single 1 and zeros that are either trailing zeros or leading zeros. They are called powers of ten because they can be formed by raising 10 to a power, like $10^3 = 10 \times 10 \times 10 = 1000$ or $10^{-2} = \frac{1}{10 \times 10} = \frac{1}{100} = 0.01$.

When a decimal is multiplied by a power of ten, the power of ten effectively shifts the decimal point of the number:
- Multiplying by 10, 100, 1000, etc. shifts the decimal point to the right. Move the decimal point one position for each zero in the power of ten. For example, $0.053 \times 100 = 5.3$ moves the decimal point 2 places to the right.
- Multiplying by 0.1, 0.01, 0.001, etc. shifts the decimal point to the left. Move the decimal point one position for each decimal place in the power of ten (including the 1). For example, $8.2 \times 0.001 = 0.0082$ moves the decimal point 3 places to the left (since there are 3 decimal digits in 0.001, including the 1).

It is sometimes necessary to add trailing or leading zeros when you shift the decimal point, like the following examples:
- $2.3 \times 1000 = 2300$ gains 2 trailing (non-decimal) zeros. Why? Multiplying by 1000 shifts the decimal point 3 places to the right, but 2.3 only has 1 decimal place, so we add $3 - 1 = 2$ zeros to the end.
- $4.9 \times 0.01 = 0.049$ gains 1 leading decimal zero. Why? Multiplying by 0.01 shifts the decimal point 2 places to the left (because 0.01 has 2 decimal digits: the 0 and the 1), but 4.9 only has 1 digit left of the decimal point, so we add $2 - 1 = 1$ zero to the front.

Example 1. $0.0076 \times 10 = 0.076$ (shift the decimal point 1 place to the right)
Example 2. $1.4 \times 100 = 140$ (shift the decimal point 2 places to the right)
Example 3. $0.85 \times 0.1 = 0.085$ (shift the decimal point 1 place to the left)
Example 4. $9.2 \times 0.001 = 0.0092$ (shift the decimal point 3 places to the left)

Master Decimals Math Practice Workbook with Answers

Exercise Set 4.1

Directions: Multiply the numbers.

1) $0.2 \times 10 =$

2) $0.7 \times 0.1 =$

3) $6.4 \times 100 =$

4) $1.8 \times 0.01 =$

5) $0.035 \times 1000 =$

6) $0.099 \times 0.001 =$

7) $27.3 \times 100 =$

8) $0.496 \times 0.1 =$

9) $0.008 \times 10 =$

10) $937 \times 0.01 =$

11) $0.016 \times 10,000 =$

12) $5.963 \times 100 =$

13) $0.01 \times 0.001 =$

14) $25 \times 0.0001 =$

15) $0.967 \times 100,000 =$

16) $0.0023 \times 1000 =$

17) $0.42 \times 0.01 =$

18) $63.84 \times 0.001 =$

19) $0.0003 \times 1,000,000 =$

20) $0.846 \times 0.00001 =$

4.2 Multiply Decimals by One-Digit Whole Numbers

To multiply a decimal by a whole number that has a single digit, follow these steps:
- First multiply the numbers like you would normally multiply whole numbers.
- Next add a decimal point in the same position as the top number. Note that this only works if the second number is a whole number. (For the case where both numbers are decimals, see Sec.'s 4.4-4.7.)
- If the answer has any decimal trailing zeros (Sec. 2.1), remove them.

Example 1. What is 2.74×3?
Since 2.74 has 2 decimal places (and since 3 is a whole number), the answer has 2 decimal places.

$$\begin{array}{r} \overset{21}{2.74} \\ \times\ 3 \\ \hline 8.22 \end{array}$$

Example 2. What is 0.638×5?
Since 0.638 has 3 decimal places (and since 5 is a whole number), the answer has 3 decimal places. However, the trailing decimal zero of 3.190 may be removed: 3.19 is equivalent to 3.190 (but 3.19 is preferred because it is simpler).

$$\begin{array}{r} \overset{14}{0.638} \\ \times\ 5 \\ \hline 3.190 \end{array}$$

Exercise Set 4.2

Directions: Multiply the numbers.

1)
$$\begin{array}{r} 7.3 \\ \times\ 6 \\ \hline \end{array}$$

2)
$$\begin{array}{r} 0.65 \\ \times\ 4 \\ \hline \end{array}$$

3)
$$\begin{array}{r} 24.1 \\ \times\ 7 \\ \hline \end{array}$$

4)
$$\begin{array}{r} 5.87 \\ \times\ 3 \\ \hline \end{array}$$

5)
   0.444
   × 3

6)
   53.6
   × 8

7)
   9.85
   × 2

8)
   0.086
   × 9

9)
   87.4
   × 5

10)
   0.906
   × 7

11)
   21.6
   × 6

12)
   34.79
   × 4

13)
   7.65
   × 2

14)
   84.3
   × 8

15)
   9.27
   × 3

16)
   0.454
   × 9

17)
   0.7416
   × 9

18)
   5.604
   × 6

19)
   24.08
   × 5

20)
   9.629
   × 7

21)
   56.38
   × 7

22)
   486.3
   × 8

23)
   5.641
   × 4

24)
   0.9078
   × 9

4.3 Multiply Decimals by Two-Digit Whole Numbers

To multiply a decimal by a whole number that has two digits, follow these steps:
- First multiply the numbers like you would normally multiply multi-digit whole numbers.
- Next add a decimal point in the same position as the top number. Note that this only works if the second number is a whole number. (For the case where both numbers are decimals, see Sec.'s 4.4-4.7.)
- If the answer has any decimal trailing zeros (Sec. 2.1), remove the trailing zeros. For example, 2.40 is equivalent to 2.4 and 16.00 is equivalent to 16.

Example 1. What is 4.7×26?

Since 4.7 has 1 decimal place (and since 26 is a whole number), the answer has 1 decimal place.

$$\begin{array}{r} \overset{\overset{1}{4}}{4.7} \\ \times\,2\,6 \\ \hline 2\,8.2 \\ 9\,4.0 \\ \hline 1\,2\,2.2 \end{array}$$

Example 2. What is 0.45×72?

Since 0.45 has 2 decimal places (and since 72 is a whole number), the answer has 2 decimal places. However, the trailing decimal zero of 32.40 may be removed: 32.4 is equivalent to 32.40 (but 32.4 is preferred because it is simpler).

$$\begin{array}{r} \overset{\overset{3}{1}}{0.45} \\ \times\,72 \\ \hline .90 \\ 31.50 \\ \hline 32.40 \end{array}$$

Exercise Set 4.3

Directions: Multiply the numbers.

1)
$$\begin{array}{r} 3.6 \\ \times\,24 \\ \hline \end{array}$$

2)
$$\begin{array}{r} 0.49 \\ \times\,53 \\ \hline \end{array}$$

3)
$$\begin{array}{r} 1.8 \\ \times\,81 \\ \hline \end{array}$$

4)
$$\begin{array}{r} 0.63 \\ \times\,74 \\ \hline \end{array}$$

5)
$$\begin{array}{r} 0.57 \\ \times\,36 \\ \hline \end{array}$$

6)
$$\begin{array}{r} 1.04 \\ \times\,16 \\ \hline \end{array}$$

7)
$$\begin{array}{r} 7.5 \\ \times\,49 \\ \hline \end{array}$$

8)
$$\begin{array}{r} 22.2 \\ \times\,90 \\ \hline \end{array}$$

9)
$$\begin{array}{r} 94.3 \\ \times\,62 \\ \hline \end{array}$$

10)
$$\begin{array}{r} 0.081 \\ \times\,78 \\ \hline \end{array}$$

11)
$$\begin{array}{r} 45.6 \\ \times\,55 \\ \hline \end{array}$$

12)
$$\begin{array}{r} 3.68 \\ \times\,27 \\ \hline \end{array}$$

4 Multiply Decimals

13)   14)   15)   16)
 6.2   0.29   0.018   7.4
×11   × 80   × 63   × 34

9/28/2023

17)   18)   19)   20)
 0.57   3.73   9.5   88.6
× 46   × 96   × 29   × 75

21)   22)   23)   24)
 4.91   0.0077   0.659   9.92
× 52   × 77   × 85   × 98

4.4 Multiply One-Digit Decimals Together

To multiply two decimals together, follow these steps:
- Count the total number of decimal places in the given numbers. For example, 0.004×0.03 has $3 + 2 = 5$ decimal places.
- Multiply the numbers like you would ordinarily multiply two whole numbers. For 0.004×0.03, for this step we get $4 \times 3 = 12$.
- Insert a decimal point such that your answer has the same number of decimal places as the answer to the first step. For example, $0.004 \times 0.03 = 0.00012$ has 5 decimal places.
- If the answer has any decimal trailing zeros (Sec. 2.1), remove the trailing zeros. For example, 0.0080 is equivalent to 0.008.

Example 1. What is 0.4×0.2?
- Step 1: 0.4×0.2 has $1 + 1 = 2$ decimal places
- Step 2: $4 \times 2 = 8$
- Step 3: Write 8 with 2 decimal places: $0.4 \times 0.2 = 0.08$

Example 2. What is 0.5×0.004?
- Step 1: 0.5×0.004 has $1 + 3 = 4$ decimal places
- Step 2: $5 \times 4 = 20$
- Step 3: Write 20 with 4 decimal places: $0.5 \times 0.004 = 0.0020$
- Step 4: Remove the trailing zero: $0.5 \times 0.004 = 0.002$

Exercise Set 4.4

Directions: Multiply the numbers.

1) $0.6 \times 0.3 =$

2) $0.2 \times 0.08 =$

3) $0.004 \times 0.7 =$

4) $0.03 \times 0.2 =$

4 Multiply Decimals

5) $0.04 \times 0.006 =$

6) $0.8 \times 0.05 =$

7) $0.5 \times 0.5 =$

8) $0.003 \times 0.3 =$

9) $0.09 \times 0.4 =$

10) $0.08 \times 0.07 =$

11) $0.2 \times 0.00002 =$

12) $0.9 \times 0.09 =$

13) $0.4 \times 0.005 =$

14) $0.0002 \times 0.06 =$

15) $0.07 \times 0.07 =$

16) $0.4 \times 0.3 =$

17) $0.004 \times 0.0002 =$

18) $0.006 \times 0.09 =$

19) $0.05 \times 0.6 =$

20) $0.0007 \times 0.0001 =$

21) $0.00009 \times 0.7 =$

22) $0.2 \times 0.06 =$

23) $0.008 \times 0.08 =$

24) $0.03 \times 0.04 =$

25) $0.7 \times 0.006 =$

26) $0.009 \times 0.008 =$

4.5 Multiply with a Decimal Square

Recall from Sec. 1.7 that a **decimal square** is a 10×10 grid where each tiny square has the value of 0.01 (one hundredth). The decimal square makes it easy to draw pictures of multiplication problems between tenths, like 0.7 × 0.5. To draw 0.7 × 0.5, shade a rectangle in the decimal square with a height of 0.7 and a width of 0.5. The answer to 0.7 × 0.5 is the area of the shaded rectangle. As shown below, there are 35 tiny squares in 0.7 × 0.5. Since each tiny square has a value of 0.01, this shows that 0.7 × 0.5 = 0.35.

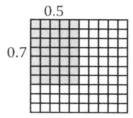

Example 1. Draw 0.4 × 0.8 on the decimal square and determine the answer.
Shade a rectangle with a height of 0.4 and a width of 0.8.

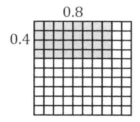

The answer is 0.4 × 0.8 = 0.32. There are 32 (out of 100) tiny squares shaded.

Example 2. Draw 0.6 × 0.3 on the decimal square and determine the answer.
Shade a rectangle with a height of 0.6 and a width of 0.3.

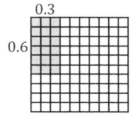

The answer is 0.6 × 0.3 = 0.18. There are 18 (out of 100) tiny squares shaded.

Exercise Set 4.5

Directions: Draw each problem on the decimal square and determine the answer.

1) $0.2 \times 0.8 =$

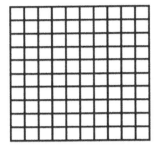

2) $0.6 \times 0.6 =$

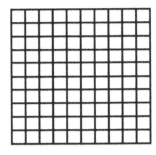

3) $0.9 \times 0.4 =$

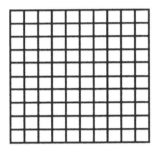

4) $0.3 \times 0.7 =$

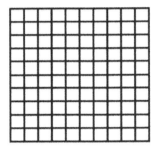

5) $0.8 \times 0.6 =$

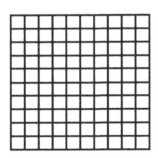

6) $0.7 \times 0.9 =$

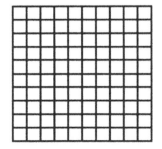

4.6 Multiply Decimals by One-Digit Decimals

Like we did in Sec. 4.4, count the total number of decimal places in the numbers being multiplied to determine the number of decimal places in the answer. (It is instructive to compare the solutions for this section with the similar problems from Sec. 4.2. The difference is that both numbers are decimals in this section, whereas one number was a whole number in Sec. 4.2. As a result, the answers to the problems in this section have more decimal places.)

Example 1. What is 0.63×0.5?

Since 0.63×0.5 has $2 + 1 = 3$ decimal places, the answer will have 3 decimal places.

$$\begin{array}{r} 0.63 \\ \times\ 0.5 \\ \hline 0.315 \end{array}$$

Example 2. What is 1.275×0.04?

Since 1.275×0.04 has $3 + 2 = 5$ decimal places, the answer will have 5 decimal places.

$$\begin{array}{r} 1.275 \\ \times\ 0.04 \\ \hline 0.05100 \end{array}$$

Now remove the trailing decimal zeros from 0.05100 to make the final answer of 0.051.

Exercise Set 4.6

Directions: Multiply the numbers.

1)
$$\begin{array}{r} 0.78 \\ \times\ 0.3 \\ \hline \end{array}$$

2)
$$\begin{array}{r} 9.4 \\ \times\ 0.06 \\ \hline \end{array}$$

3)
$$\begin{array}{r} 0.465 \\ \times\ 0.4 \\ \hline \end{array}$$

4)
$$\begin{array}{r} 2.17 \\ \times\ 0.007 \\ \hline \end{array}$$

4 Multiply Decimals

5) 52.6 × 0.08

6) 0.383 × 0.2

7) 1.97 × 0.005

8) 0.0648 × 0.9

9) 8.02 × 0.1

10) 22.2 × 0.0007

11) 0.925 × 0.06

12) 404.7 × 0.3

13) 142.9 × 0.04

14) 6.308 × 0.9

15) 0.5915 × 0.008

16) 37.72 × 0.05

17) 0.4593 × 0.06

18) 0.08296 × 0.002

19) 20.71 × 0.3

20) 7.804 × 0.001

21) 0.003162 × 0.5

22) 55.55 × 0.08

23) 6.439 × 0.007

24) 963.7 × 0.9

4.7 Multiply Decimals by Two-Digit Decimals

Like we did in Sec. 4.4, count the total number of decimal places in the numbers being multiplied to determine the number of decimal places in the answer. (It is instructive to compare the solutions for this section with the similar problems from Sec. 4.3. The difference is that both numbers are decimals in this section, whereas one number was a whole number in Sec. 4.3. As a result, the answers to the problems in this section have more decimal places.)

Example 1. What is 6.3×2.4?
Since 6.3×2.4 has $1 + 1 = 2$ decimal places, the answer will have 2 decimal places.

$$\begin{array}{r} \overset{1}{6.3} \\ \times\,2.4 \\ \hline 2.5\,2 \\ 1\,2.6\,0 \\ \hline 1\,5.1\,2 \end{array}$$

Example 2. What is 0.46×0.35?
Since 0.46×0.35 has $2 + 2 = 4$ decimal places, the answer will have 4 decimal places.

$$\begin{array}{r} \overset{1}{\underset{3}{}} \\ 0.4\,6 \\ \times\,0.3\,5 \\ \hline 0.0\,2\,3\,0 \\ 0.1\,3\,8\,0 \\ \hline 0.1\,6\,1\,0 \end{array}$$

Now remove the trailing decimal zero from 0.1610 to make the final answer of 0.161.

Example 3. What is 2.73×4.8?
Since 2.73×4.8 has $2 + 1 = 3$ decimal places, the answer will have 3 decimal places.

$$\begin{array}{r} \overset{2\ \ 1}{\underset{5\ \ 2}{}} \\ 2.7\,3 \\ \times\,4.8 \\ \hline 2.1\,8\,4 \\ 1\,0.9\,2\,0 \\ \hline 1\,3.1\,0\,4 \end{array}$$

Exercise Set 4.7

Directions: Multiply the numbers.

1)

$$\begin{array}{r} 7.4 \\ \times\ 5.3 \\ \hline \end{array}$$

2)

$$\begin{array}{r} 0.8\,3 \\ \times\ 0.2\,6 \\ \hline \end{array}$$

3)

$$\begin{array}{r} 0.5\,9 \\ \times\ 7.4 \\ \hline \end{array}$$

4)

$$\begin{array}{r} 3.6 \\ \times\ 0.0\,1\,1 \\ \hline \end{array}$$

5)

$$\begin{array}{r} 4.1 \\ \times\ 0.6\,2 \\ \hline \end{array}$$

6)

$$\begin{array}{r} 0.0\,2\,5 \\ \times\ 3.8 \\ \hline \end{array}$$

7)

$$\begin{array}{r} 0.1\,8 \\ \times\ 0.0\,9\,4 \\ \hline \end{array}$$

8)

$$\begin{array}{r} 9\,6.7 \\ \times\ 8.5 \\ \hline \end{array}$$

9)

$$\begin{array}{r} 6.5\,2 \\ \times\ 0.0\,0\,4\,4 \\ \hline \end{array}$$

10)

$$\begin{array}{r} 0.3\,0\,8 \\ \times\ 0.0\,1\,9 \\ \hline \end{array}$$

11)

$$\begin{array}{r} 7.6\,7 \\ \times\ 0.5\,7 \\ \hline \end{array}$$

12)

$$\begin{array}{r} 3.6\,8 \\ \times\ 2.6 \\ \hline \end{array}$$

Master Decimals Math Practice Workbook with Answers

13) 0.055
$\times 7.5$

14) 9.3
$\times 0.93$

15) 0.0044
$\times 4.8$

16) 0.26
$\times 0.61$

17) 0.0019
$\times 0.37$

18) 8.1
$\times 6.2$

19) 0.0688
$\times 0.083$

20) 4.27
$\times 0.0099$

21) 0.392
$\times 0.0018$

22) 0.746
$\times 0.054$

23) 9.85
$\times 2.6$

24) 0.00834
$\times 0.047$

4.8 The Distributive Property

According to the **distributive property** of arithmetic:
$$a \times (b + c) = a \times b + a \times c$$
The formula above applies for any possible numbers for a, b, and c. For example, if $a = 3$, $b = 4$, and $c = 6$, the left-hand side of the equation is $a \times (b + c) = 3 \times (4 + 6) = 3 \times 10 = 30$ and the right-hand side of the equation is $a \times b + a \times c = 3 \times 4 + 3 \times 6 = 12 + 18 = 30$. In this case, both sides of the equation equal 30. If you try any other values for a, b, and c, both sides of the equation will be equal (though they may both equal some other value besides 30). Try it!

The distributive property may also be expressed in the following form:
$$(b + c) \times a = b \times a + c \times a$$
To get the above form, we applied the **commutative property** of arithmetic, meaning that the order in which numbers are multiplied does not matter. For example, $4 \times 3 = 3 \times 4$. This means that $a \times b = b \times a$, $a \times c = c \times a$, and $a \times (b + c) = (b + c) \times a$.

Note that the distributive property can be extended to include additional terms. For example:
$$a \times (b + c + d) = a \times b + a \times c + a \times d$$

The distributive property can be used to multiply decimals by one-digit numbers. For example, consider the problem 0.6×2.4. If we let $a = 0.6$, $b = 2$, and $c = 0.4$ in the formula at the top of the page, we get:
$$0.6 \times (2 + 0.4) = 0.6 \times 2 + 0.6 \times 0.4$$
The left-hand side is 0.6×2.4 and the right-hand side can be simplified:
$$0.6 \times 2.4 = 1.2 + 0.24 = 1.44$$
Here, we have applied the distributive property to show that $0.6 \times 2.4 = 1.44$. If we apply the method from Sec. 4.6, we get the same answer:

$$\begin{array}{r} \overset{2}{2.4} \\ \times\ 0.6 \\ \hline 1.44 \end{array}$$

$$a \times (b + c) = a \times b + a \times c$$
$$a \times (b + c + d) = a \times b + a \times c + a \times d$$
$$(b + c) \times a = b \times a + c \times a$$

Example 1. Apply the distributive property to determine 0.3×4.1.

First write $4.1 = 4 + 0.1$. This is the expanded form of 4.1 (recall Sec. 1.4).

Let $a = 0.3$, $b = 4$, and $c = 0.1$ in $a \times (b + c) = a \times b + a \times c$:

$$0.3 \times 4.1 = 0.3 \times (4 + 0.1) = 0.3 \times 4 + 0.3 \times 0.1 = 1.2 + 0.03 = 1.23$$

Example 2. Apply the distributive property to determine 2×3.54.

First write $3.54 = 3 + 0.5 + 0.04$. This is the expanded form of 3.54 (recall Sec. 1.4). For this example, we will use the second equation from the top of the page.

Let $a = 2$, $b = 3$, $c = 0.5$, and $d = 0.04$ in $a \times (b + c + d) = a \times b + a \times c + a \times d$:

$$2 \times 3.54 = 2 \times (3 + 0.5 + 0.04) = 2 \times 3 + 2 \times 0.5 + 2 \times 0.04 = 6 + 1 + 0.08 = 7.08$$

Example 3. Apply the distributive property to determine 4.5×0.06.

First write $4.5 = 4 + 0.5$. This is the expanded form of 4.5 (recall Sec. 1.4). For this example, we will use the third equation from the top of the page.

Let $a = 0.06$, $b = 4$, and $c = 0.5$ in $(b + c) \times a = b \times a + c \times a$:

$$4.5 \times 0.06 = (4 + 0.5) \times 0.06 = 4 \times 0.06 + 0.5 \times 0.06 = 0.24 + 0.030 = 0.27$$

Exercise Set 4.8

Directions: Apply the distributive property to determine each answer.

1) $0.8 \times 7.6 =$

2) $5 \times 4.9 =$

3) $0.6 \times 0.37 =$

4 Multiply Decimals

4) $0.04 \times 5.2 =$

5) $0.002 \times 0.61 =$

6) $9.7 \times 8 =$

7) $0.48 \times 0.5 =$

8) $0.072 \times 0.03 =$

9) $4 \times 6.57 =$

10) $0.9 \times 0.192 =$

11) $0.08 \times 7.33 =$

12) $63.4 \times 0.5 =$

4.9 Multiply Decimals in Expanded Form

If two-digit decimals multiply one another, like 2.6 × 1.4 or like 0.75 × 0.032 (where both numbers have two consecutive nonzero digits), we can multiply the numbers in expanded form (Sec. 1.4) if we think of the problem as finding the area of a rectangle. For example, we may think of 2.6 × 1.4 as the area of a rectangle where the length is 2.6 and the width is 1.4.

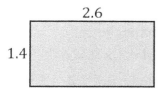

In expanded form (Sec. 1.4), the length is 2 + 0.6 and the width is 1 + 0.4. When we express the length and width in expanded form, this divides the rectangle into four smaller rectangles, as shown below.

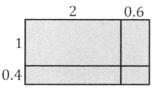

The area of the original rectangle equals the sum of the areas of the four smaller rectangles. If we find the area of the four small rectangles, we can add them up to determine the area of the original rectangle.

- area of the top left rectangle: 2 × 1 = 2
- area of the top right rectangle: 0.6 × 1 = 0.6
- area of the bottom left rectangle: 2 × 0.4 = 0.8
- area of the bottom right rectangle: 0.6 × 0.4 = 0.24

The total area is 2 + 0.6 + 0.8 + 0.24 = 3.64. Since the area of the original rectangle is 2.6 × 1.4, we have shown that 2.6 × 1.4 = 3.64. If we apply the method from Sec. 4.7, we get the same answer:

$$\begin{array}{r} \overset{2}{}2.6 \\ \times\ 1.4 \\ \hline 1.04 \\ 2.60 \\ \hline 3.64 \end{array}$$

4 Multiply Decimals

Example 1. Apply the area method to determine 3.7×2.5.

Draw a rectangle with a length of $3 + 0.7$ and a width of $2 + 0.5$.

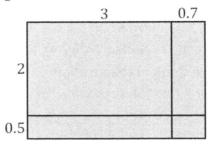

Find the area of the four small rectangles:
- area of the top left rectangle: $3 \times 2 = 6$
- area of the top right rectangle: $0.7 \times 2 = 1.4$
- area of the bottom left rectangle: $3 \times 0.5 = 1.5$
- area of the bottom right rectangle: $0.7 \times 0.5 = 0.35$

Add these areas together:
$$3.7 \times 2.5 = 6 + 1.4 + 1.5 + 0.35 = 9.25$$

Exercise Set 4.9

Directions: Apply the area method to determine each answer.

1) $1.8 \times 1.4 =$

2) $4.7 \times 3.6 =$

3) $7.5 \times 8.2 =$

4) $9.3 \times 0.81 =$

5) $0.64 \times 0.29 =$

6) $58 \times 0.44 =$

7) $0.037 \times 0.52 =$

4.10 Multiplication Word Problems

The word problems in this section involve multiplying decimals (and may also involve addition or subtraction).

Example 1. Eileen earns $8.25 per hour. How much money will Eileen earn for 40 hours of work?

Multiply $8.25 by 40:

$$\begin{array}{r} {\scriptstyle 1\ \ 2} \\ \$8.25 \\ \times\ 40 \\ \hline 0 \\ \$330.00 \\ \hline \$330.00 \end{array}$$

Eileen will earn $330.

Exercise Set 4.10

Directions: Determine the answer to each word problem.

1) A video game store offers a store credit of $5.49 for each used game that customers trade in. If a customer trades in three used games, how much credit will the customer receive?

2) A medium egg weighs approximately 1.75 ounces. How much does a dozen medium eggs weigh?

3) A postcard is 5.5 inches wide and 3.75 inches tall. What is the area of the postcard?

4) A software company offers customers a monthly subscription for $4.95 per month and an annual subscription for $49.95 per year. How much do customers save each year when they purchase an annual subscription instead of a monthly subscription?

5) A store sells apples for $0.54 each and oranges for $0.68 each. How much does it cost to buy 6 apples and 9 oranges (if there is no sales tax)?

6) If an ant crawls in a straight line with a constant speed of 0.24 m/s, how far will the ant travel in 3.8 s?

7) A particular car travels 24.5 miles per gallon, on average. About how far can the car travel with 13.2 gallons of gasoline in its gas tank?

4.11 Exponents of Decimals

An expression of the form 0.1^3 has a **base** and an **exponent** (also called the **power**). In 0.1^3, the number 0.1 is the base and the number 3 is the exponent (or power). The exponent indicates the number of times that the base multiplies itself. For example, $0.1^3 = 0.1 \times 0.1 \times 0.1$ has three 0.1's multiplied together.

If the exponent equals 2, it is called a **square**. For example, $0.3^2 = 0.3 \times 0.3 = 0.09$ is "0.3 squared." If the exponent equals 3, it is called a **cube**. For example, $0.1^3 = 0.1 \times 0.1 \times 0.1 = 0.001$ is "0.1 cubed." An exponent of 1 does nothing. For example, $0.7^1 = 0.7$. (For curious minds, when a nonzero base is raised to an exponent of 0, the answer is 1, regardless of the base. For example, $0.9^0 = 1$ and $0.1^0 = 1$. Why? Consider $\frac{2^5}{2^2} = \frac{2 \times 2 \times 2 \times 2 \times 2}{2 \times 2} = \frac{32}{4} = 8 = 2^3$. You can show in general that $\frac{x^a}{x^b} = x^{a-b}$. For the case $a = b$, you get $\frac{x^a}{x^a} = x^{a-a}$ which simplifies to $1 = x^0$.)

Example 1. $0.4^2 = 0.4 \times 0.4 = 0.16$
Example 2. $0.2^3 = 0.2 \times 0.2 \times 0.2 = 0.04 \times 0.2 = 0.008$
Example 3. $0.1^4 = 0.1 \times 0.1 \times 0.1 \times 0.1 = 0.01 \times 0.01 = 0.0001$

Exercise Set 4.11

Directions: Use repeated multiplication to determine each answer.

1) $0.7^2 =$

2) $0.4^3 =$

3) $0.05^2 =$

4) $0.6^3 =$

5) $0.8^2 =$

6) $0.3^4 =$

7) $0.2^5 =$

8) $0.01^3 =$

9) $1.4^2 =$

10) $0.5^3 =$

11) $0.04^4 =$

12) $0.06^3 =$

13) $0.27^2 =$

14) $0.1^5 =$

15) $0.002^3 =$

16) $0.015^2 =$

17) $0.8^3 =$

18) $0.07^3 =$

19) $1.4^3 =$

Master Decimals Math Practice Workbook with Answers

4.12 Square Roots of Decimals

The **radical** symbol ($\sqrt{\ }$) indicates a **square root**. For example, $\sqrt{0.04}$ means, "Which number squared is equal to 0.04?" This is equivalent to asking, "Which number times itself is equal to 0.04?" The positive answer is $\sqrt{0.04} = 0.2$ because $0.2 \times 0.2 = 0.04$.

Example 1. What is the positive answer to $\sqrt{0.09}$?
The positive answer is $\sqrt{0.09} = 0.3$ because $0.3 \times 0.3 = 0.09$.

Exercise Set 4.12

Directions: Determine the positive answer to each square root.

1) $\sqrt{0.25} =$

2) $\sqrt{0.0001} =$

3) $\sqrt{0.81} =$

4) $\sqrt{0.0004} =$

5) $\sqrt{1.44} =$

6) $\sqrt{0.0036} =$

7) $\sqrt{0.0225} =$

8) $\sqrt{0.64} =$

9) $\sqrt{0.000009} =$

10) $\sqrt{1.21} =$

11) $\sqrt{0.000625} =$

12) $\sqrt{0.00000001} =$

4.13 Decimal Calculations

When a calculation combines addition, subtraction, and multiplication, follow these rules to determine which operation to perform first:
- If there are parentheses, do the arithmetic inside of the parentheses first. For example, the parentheses in $0.4 \times (2 + 3)$ instruct us to add $2 + 3 = 5$ before we multiply: $0.4 \times (2 + 3) = 0.4 \times 5 = 2$.
- If there are exponents, evaluate the exponents next. For example, the exponent in $9.5 - 3^2$ tells us to square 3 before we subtract: $9.5 - 3^2 = 9.5 - 9 = 0.5$.
- Multiply before you add or subtract (except when parentheses require you to add or subtract first). For example, since $1.3 + 4 \times 2$ does not have parentheses, we multiply before we add: $1.3 + 4 \times 2 = 1.3 + 8 = 9.3$. (For calculations that also involve division, see Chapter 5.)
- Save addition and subtraction for last (except when parentheses require you to add or subtract earlier). When adding and subtracting, work left to right.

The abbreviation PEMDAS can help you remember the order of operations: P stands for Parentheses, E stands for Exponents, MD stands for Multiplication/Division from left to right, and AS stands for Addition/Subtraction from left to right.

Example 1. Evaluate $(7 - 3) \times (1.8 + 3.7)$.
Do math in parentheses first: $(7 - 3) \times (1.8 + 3.7) = 4 \times 5.5 = \boxed{22}$

Example 2. Evaluate $0.3^2 - 0.2^3$.
Evaluate the exponents before subtracting: $0.3^2 - 0.2^3 = 0.09 - 0.008 = \boxed{0.082}$

Example 3. Evaluate $17 - 4 \times 3.2$.
We must multiply before we subtract (since there are no parentheses): $17 - 4 \times 3.2$
$= 17 - 12.8 = \boxed{4.2}$

Example 4. Evaluate $(6.5 - 5) \times 4 + 2^2$.
Do math in parentheses first: $(6.5 - 5) \times 4 + 2^2 = 1.5 \times 4 + 2^2$
Evaluate the exponent next: $1.5 \times 4 + 2^2 = 1.5 \times 4 + 4$
We must multiply before we add (since there are no parentheses): $1.5 \times 4 + 4 = 6 + 4$
Add and subtract last (except when parentheses instruct otherwise): $6 + 4 = \boxed{10}$

4 Multiply Decimals

Exercise Set 4.13

Directions: Follow the rules on the previous page to determine the answers.

1) $7 \times (5.3 - 1.6) =$

2) $8.3 - 0.2 \times 4.9 =$

3) $1.8^2 + 0.9^2 =$

4) $(0.5 + 0.36) \times (2 - 0.7) =$

5) $0.6 \times 0.45 - 0.9 \times (0.04 + 0.08) =$

6) $1.3 + 0.7 \times 0.2 + 0.8 =$

7) $0.4^2 - 0.05 \times 1.7 =$

8) $(7 \times 0.4 - 0.9)^2 =$

4.14 Scientific Notation

In scientific notation, a power of ten is used to position the decimal point immediately after the first digit of a number, like 7.24×10^5 or 4.315×10^{-9}. (It may help to review Sec. 4.1.)

If a number equals 10 or larger, to express the number in scientific notation, multiply by a positive power of ten and shift the decimal point to the left the same number of decimal places as the exponent. For example, $63,800 = 6.38 \times 10^4$ (where, as usual, we removed the decimal trailing zeros). It may help to think of 63,800 as 63,800.0 to see where the decimal point was originally.

If a number is less than 1, to express the number in scientific notation, multiply by a negative power of ten and shift the decimal point to the right the same number of decimal places as the exponent. For example, $0.0052 = 5.2 \times 10^{-3}$.

Example 1. $3592 = 3.592 \times 10^3$ We moved the decimal point 3 places to the left.
Example 2. $0.068 = 6.8 \times 10^{-2}$ We moved the decimal point 2 places to the right.
Example 3. $183,000 = 1.83 \times 10^5$ We moved the decimal point 5 places to the left.

Exercise Set 4.14

Directions: Express each number in scientific notation.

1) $578 =$

2) $0.067 =$

3) $0.000268 =$

4) $35,200 =$

4 Multiply Decimals

5) $0.004276 =$

6) $145.54 =$

7) $786,000 =$

8) $0.00000964 =$

9) $0.32 =$

10) $7689.2 =$

11) $1,400,000 =$

12) $0.0005 =$

13) $0.088 =$

14) $42,300 =$

15) $365,400,000 =$

16) $0.000000096 =$

17) $0.0000421 =$

18) $23,000,000 =$

5 DIVIDE DECIMALS

$$\begin{array}{r} 0.34 \\ 6{\overline{\smash{\big)}\,2.04}} \\ \underline{1.8} \\ 0.24 \end{array}$$

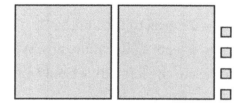

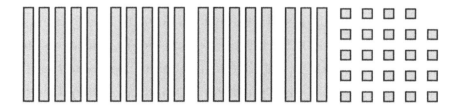

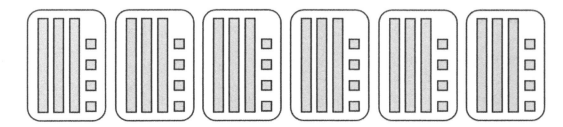

5 Divide Decimals

5.1 Divide Decimals by Powers of Ten

The strategy for dividing by a power of ten is similar to the strategy for multiplying by a power of ten (Sec. 4.1); the only difference is that the decimal point is shifted in the opposite direction.

- Dividing by 10, 100, 1000, etc. shifts the decimal point to the left. Move the decimal point one position for each zero in the power of ten. For example, $0.82 \div 100 = 0.0082$ moves the decimal point two places to the left.
- Dividing by 0.1, 0.01, 0.001, etc. shifts the decimal point to the right. Move the decimal point one position for each decimal place in the power of ten (including the 1). For example, $0.47 \div 0.001 = 470$ moves the decimal point 3 places to the right (since there are 3 decimal digits in 0.001, including the 1).

It is sometimes necessary to add trailing or leading zeros when you shift the decimal point, like the following examples:

- $3.9 \div 0.001 = 3900$ gains 2 trailing (non-decimal) zeros. Why? Dividing by 0.001 shifts the decimal point 3 places to the right, but 3.9 only has 1 decimal place, so we add $3 - 1 = 2$ zeros to the end.
- $5.1 \div 100 = 0.051$ gains 1 leading decimal zero. Why? Dividing by 100 shifts the decimal point 2 places to the left, but 5.1 only has 1 digit left of the decimal point, so we add $2 - 1 = 1$ zero to the front.

Example 1. $0.026 \div 10 = 0.0026$ (shift the decimal point 1 place to the left)
Example 2. $0.73 \div 1000 = 0.00073$ (shift the decimal point 3 places to the left)
Example 3. $0.0048 \div 0.1 = 0.048$ (shift the decimal point 1 place to the right)
Example 4. $0.055 \div 0.001 = 55$ (shift the decimal point 3 places to the right)

Exercise Set 5.1

Directions: Divide the numbers.

1) $38.9 \div 100 =$

2) $0.0096 \div 0.01 =$

3) $7.2 \div 10 =$

4) $0.16 \div 0.001 =$

5) $0.028 \div 0.0001 =$

6) $0.47 \div 100 =$

7) $8.6 \div 0.1 =$

8) $0.496 \div 1000 =$

9) $0.00101 \div 10{,}000 =$

10) $25.4 \div 0.01 =$

11) $0.052 \div 100 =$

12) $9.74 \div 0.00001 =$

13) $3.5 \div 0.001 =$

14) $473 \div 100{,}000 =$

15) $96.7 \div 1000 =$

16) $0.0793 \div 0.1 =$

17) $0.0063 \div 0.000001 =$

18) $5400 \div 1{,}000{,}000 =$

19) $0.75 \div 0.01 =$

20) $0.00888 \div 0.0000001 =$

21) $49{,}300 \div 10{,}000{,}000 =$

22) $0.042637 \div 0.001 =$

23) $4.15 \div 100 =$

24) $0.006 \div 0.00001 =$

5.2 Divide Decimals by One-Digit Whole Numbers

The dividend divided by the divisor is equal to the quotient. For example, in $0.6 \div 4 = 0.15$, the **dividend** is 0.6, the **divisor** is 4, and the **quotient** is 0.15.

You can divide decimals using the method of long division. This works very much like long division with whole numbers, with a few exceptions:
- The position of the decimal point is important. Keep the decimal point in the same position throughout the solution.
- When a step requires multiplying numbers, use what we learned in Chapter 4 to determine the answer to the multiplication.
- If you need additional digits, you may add trailing decimal zeros to the dividend. For example, 0.6 is equivalent to 0.60 and 0.600. The additional decimal zeros are sometimes helpful.
- If the answer has decimal trailing zeros, remove them (Sec. 2.1).

Example 1. What is $0.81 \div 3$?
Write the dividend (0.81) inside of the long division symbol and the divisor (3) to the left of the long division symbol.

$$3 \overline{) 0.81}$$

What is the largest decimal with a single nonzero digit that you can multiply by 3 such that the product does not exceed 0.81? Since $3 \times 0.2 = 0.6$ is less than 0.81 and since $3 \times 0.3 = 0.9$ is greater than 0.81, write 0.2 at the top and write 0.6 below 0.8.

$$\begin{array}{r} 0.2 \\ 3 \overline{) 0.81} \\ 0.6 \end{array}$$

Subtract 0.6 from 0.81. We get $0.81 - 0.6 = 0.21$. What can we multiply 3 by to make 0.21? Since $3 \times 0.07 = 0.21$, write a 7 in the hundredths place at the top.

$$\begin{array}{r} 0.27 \\ 3 \overline{) 0.81} \\ \underline{0.6 } \\ 0.21 \end{array}$$

The answer is $0.81 \div 3 = 0.27$.

Master Decimals Math Practice Workbook with Answers

Example 2. What is $2.5 \div 4$?

Write the dividend (2.5) inside of the long division symbol and the divisor (4) to the left of the long division symbol.

$$4\overline{)2.5}$$

What is the largest decimal with a single nonzero digit that you can multiply by 4 such that the product does not exceed 2.5? Since $4 \times 0.6 = 2.4$ is less than 2.5 and since $4 \times 0.7 = 2.8$ is greater than 2.5, write 0.6 at the top and write 2.4 below 2.5.

$$\begin{array}{r} 0.6 \\ 4\overline{)2.5} \\ 2.4 \end{array}$$

Subtract 2.4 from 2.5. We get $2.5 - 2.4 = 0.1$. Add a trailing zero to 2.5 to make 2.50 and bring the zero down to turn 0.1 into 0.10. We will need this additional digit for the next step. (Compare and contrast this example with the previous example.)

$$\begin{array}{r} 0.6 \\ 4\overline{)2.50} \\ \underline{2.4} \\ 0.10 \end{array}$$

What is the largest decimal with a single nonzero digit that you can multiply by 4 such that the product does not exceed 0.10? Since $4 \times 0.02 = 0.08$ is less than 0.10 and since $4 \times 0.03 = 0.12$ is greater than 0.10, add a 2 to the hundredths place at the top and write 0.08 below 0.10. See the left diagram below.

$$\begin{array}{r} 0.62 \\ 4\overline{)2.50} \\ 2.4 \\ 0.10 \\ \underline{0.08} \end{array} \qquad \begin{array}{r} 0.625 \\ 4\overline{)2.500} \\ 2.4 \\ 0.10 \\ \underline{0.08} \\ 0.020 \end{array}$$

Subtract 0.08 from 0.10. We get $0.10 - 0.08 = 0.02$. Add a trailing zero to 2.50 to make 2.500 and bring the zero down to turn 0.02 into 0.020. We will use this additional digit in the next step. What can we multiply 4 by to make 0.020? Since $4 \times 0.005 = 0.020$, write a 5 in the thousandths place at the top. See the right diagram above. The answer is $2.5 \div 4 = 0.625$.

Tip: Check your answers by multiplying. For example, $4 \times 0.625 = 2.5$.

5 Divide Decimals

Exercise Set 5.2

Directions: Divide the numbers.

1) $5 \overline{) 3.65}$

2) $2 \overline{) 0.92}$

3) $9 \overline{) 56.7}$

4) $6 \overline{) 1.404}$

5) $4 \overline{) 0.18}$

6) $8 \overline{) 0.0728}$

7) $3 \overline{) 8.4}$

8) $7 \overline{) 0.1022}$

9) $6 \overline{) 52.2}$

10) $7 \overline{) 4.459}$

11) $5 \overline{) 1.11}$

12) $2 \overline{) 0.75}$

13) $9\overline{)0.846}$

14) $3\overline{)0.0174}$

15) $8\overline{)1.88}$

16) $4\overline{)2.452}$

17) $8\overline{)0.0028}$

18) $5\overline{)0.31}$

19) $2\overline{)15.268}$

20) $6\overline{)0.528}$

21) $7\overline{)4.501}$

22) $3\overline{)0.0237}$

23) $4\overline{)0.25}$

24) $9\overline{)0.01287}$

5.3 Divide Decimals by Two-Digit Whole Numbers

The problems in this section have divisors that are double-digit whole numbers. The strategy from Sec. 5.2 works to solve these problems.

Example 1. What is $9.62 \div 26$?

Write the dividend (9.62) inside of the long division symbol and the divisor (26) to the left of the long division symbol.

$$26\overline{)9.62}$$

What is the largest decimal with a single nonzero digit that you can multiply by 26 such that the product does not exceed 9.62? Since $26 \times 0.3 = 7.8$ is less than 9.62 and since $26 \times 0.4 = 10.4$ is greater than 9.62, write 0.3 at the top and write 7.8 below 9.6.

$$\begin{array}{r} 0.3 \\ 26\overline{)9.62} \\ 7.8 \end{array}$$

Subtract 7.8 from 9.62. We get $9.62 - 7.8 = 1.82$. What can we multiply 26 by to make 1.82? Since $26 \times 0.07 = 1.82$, write a 7 in the hundredths place at the top.

$$\begin{array}{r} 0.37 \\ 26\overline{)9.62} \\ \underline{7.8} \\ 1.82 \end{array}$$

The answer is $9.62 \div 26 = 0.37$. Check the answer by multiplying: $26 \times 0.37 = 9.62$.

Exercise Set 5.3

Directions: Divide the numbers.

1) $36\overline{)15.12}$

2) $54\overline{)3.78}$

3) $72\overline{)453.6}$

4) $18\overline{)0.117}$

5) 61)18.3

6) 49)34.888

7) 27)0.675

8) 93)0.372

9) 55)445.5

10) 80)38.8

11) 34)57.8

12) 62)5.952

13) 13)8.32

14) 28)2.03

15) 41)0.3403

16) 76)323.76

5.4 Divide with Base-10 Blocks

We can use base-10 blocks to draw pictures of decimals divided by whole numbers. Recall from Sec. 1.7 that:
- a large square represents a single unit
- a strip represents 0.1
- a tiny square represents 0.01

Follow these steps to draw a decimal divided by a whole number:
- Draw large squares, strips, and tiny squares that add up to the dividend. For example, in 1.38 ÷ 6 the dividend is 1.38 (and the divisor is 6). Draw one large square plus 3 strips plus 8 tiny squares to make 1.38.
- What is the divisor? This is how many groups you need to make. Rearrange the large squares, strips, and tiny squares into this many groups, where each group has the same value. It is usually necessary to regroup in order to do this.
- Regroup, if needed. One large square can be redrawn as 10 strips. One strip can be redrawn as 10 tiny squares.
- Once all of the large squares, strips, and tiny squares have been used, you have the desired number of groups, and each group has the same value, the value of each group is the answer (called the quotient) to the problem.

Example 1. Use base-10 blocks to determine 1.38 ÷ 6.

The dividend is 1.38. Draw one large square, 3 strips, and 8 tiny squares to draw 1.38.

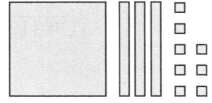

The divisor is 6. We wish to rearrange the squares and strips to make 6 equal groups. In order to do this, we need to regroup. We will redraw the large square as 10 strips and we will redraw one strip as 10 tiny squares. There are now 12 strips and 18 tiny squares (see the next page). As a check, this still equals 1.38.

Master Decimals Math Practice Workbook with Answers

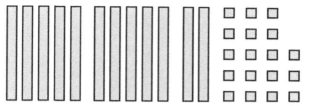

To make 6 equals groups, we will put 2 strips and 3 tiny squares in each group.

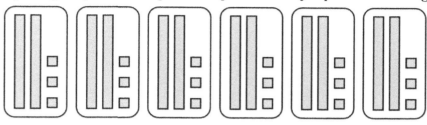

Now 6 equal groups have been formed by rearranging (and regrouping) the base-10 blocks from the dividend. The answer equals the value of each group. Since each group has 2 strips and 3 tiny squares, the answer is 0.23.

Exercise Set 5.4

Directions: Use base-10 blocks to determine each answer.

1) $2.24 \div 7$

2) 6.15 ÷ 5

3) 3.2 ÷ 8

5.5 One-Digit Divisors and Quotients

The problems in this section are similar to division facts, except that some numbers are decimals. The divisors and quotients have a single nonzero digit, but the dividend may have two nonzero digits, like $0.018 \div 0.3 = 0.06$. One way to find the answer is to ask which number with a single nonzero digit can be multiplied by the divisor in order to make the dividend. Carry out the multiplication (like we did in Chapter 4) to check the answer. For example, $0.018 \div 0.3$ asks, "Which number with one nonzero digit can you multiply by 0.3 to make 0.018?" The answer is 0.06 because $0.3 \times 0.06 = 0.018$ (since $3 \times 6 = 18$ and since 0.3×0.06 has a total of 3 decimal places).

Example 1. $2.4 \div 8 = 0.3$ because $8 \times 0.3 = 2.4$.
Example 2. $0.15 \div 0.03 = 5$ because $0.03 \times 5 = 0.15$.
Example 3. $0.03 \div 0.6 = 0.05$ because $0.6 \times 0.05 = 0.030 = 0.03$.

Exercise Set 5.5

Directions: Divide the numbers.

1) $0.12 \div 0.4 =$

2) $1.6 \div 0.2 =$

3) $0.025 \div 0.5 =$

4) $0.28 \div 0.04 =$

5) $3.6 \div 9 =$

6) $0.01 \div 0.05 =$

7) $0.006 \div 0.002 =$

8) $0.32 \div 40 =$

9) $81 \div 900 =$

10) $0.024 \div 0.4 =$

5 Divide Decimals

11) $0.21 \div 0.03 =$

12) $0.2 \div 0.4 =$

13) $0.4 \div 0.2 =$

14) $0.072 \div 0.9 =$

15) $4.8 \div 6 =$

16) $0.0032 \div 0.8 =$

17) $0.005 \div 0.01 =$

18) $0.42 \div 0.007 =$

19) $4.5 \div 5 =$

20) $0.027 \div 0.0009 =$

21) $0.64 \div 0.8 =$

22) $0.06 \div 0.02 =$

23) $0.0054 \div 0.006 =$

24) $24 \div 0.3 =$

25) $0.28 \div 0.04 =$

26) $0.16 \div 8 =$

27) $0.00056 \div 0.7 =$

28) $0.02 \div 0.05 =$

29) $0.045 \div 0.09 =$

30) $0.12 \div 2 =$

31) $0.36 \div 0.006 =$

32) $72 \div 0.008 =$

5.6 Divide by One-Digit Decimals

The divisors in this section are decimals with one nonzero digit. The same strategy that we applied in Sec. 5.2 works to solve these problems.

Example 1. What is $0.148 \div 0.4$?
Write the dividend (0.148) inside of the long division symbol and the divisor (0.4) to the left of the long division symbol.

$$0.4 \overline{)0.148}$$

What is the largest number with a single nonzero digit that you can multiply by 0.4 such that the product does not exceed 0.148? Since $0.4 \times 0.3 = 0.12$ is less than 0.148 and since $0.4 \times 0.4 = 0.16$ is greater than 0.148, write 0.3 at the top and write 0.12 below 0.14.

$$\begin{array}{r} 0.3 \\ 0.4 \overline{)0.148} \\ 0.12 \end{array}$$

Subtract 0.12 from 0.148. We get $0.148 - 0.12 = 0.028$. What can we multiply 0.4 by to make 0.028? Since $0.4 \times 0.07 = 0.028$, write a 7 in the hundredths place at the top.

$$\begin{array}{r} 0.37 \\ 0.4 \overline{)0.148} \\ 0.12 \\ 0.28 \end{array}$$

The answer is $0.148 \div 0.4 = 0.37$. Check the answer by multiplying: $0.4 \times 0.37 = 0.148$.

Exercise Set 5.6

Directions: Divide the numbers.

1) $0.4 \overline{)0.304}$

2) $0.6 \overline{)4.92}$

3) $0.03 \overline{)0.0048}$

4) $0.7 \overline{)0.0175}$

5 Divide Decimals

5) $0.05 \overline{)0.46}$

6) $0.2 \overline{)7.62}$

7) $0.009 \overline{)0.756}$

8) $0.1 \overline{)0.000038}$

9) $0.8 \overline{)49.6}$

10) $0.07 \overline{)0.0665}$

11) $0.6 \overline{)0.402}$

12) $0.05 \overline{)18.2}$

13) $0.009 \overline{)0.639}$

14) $0.1 \overline{)0.303}$

15) $0.08 \overline{)2.16}$

16) $0.2 \overline{)0.1984}$

17) 0.03)0.0654

18) 0.6)0.0474

19) 0.4)0.34

20) 0.07)129.64

21) 0.2)0.00176

22) 0.05)3.08

23) 0.9)0.5436

24) 0.001)0.0427

25) 0.07)2.072

26) 0.4)0.0212

27) 0.06)0.9894

28) 0.8)0.000368

5.7 Divide by Two-Digit Decimals

The divisors in this section are decimals with two nonzero digits. The same strategy that we applied in Sec. 5.3 works to solve these problems.

Example 1. What is $2.392 \div 0.52$?
Write the dividend (2.392) inside of the long division symbol and the divisor (0.52) to the left of the long division symbol.

$$0.52\overline{)2.392}$$

What is the largest number with a single nonzero digit that you can multiply by 0.52 such that the product does not exceed 2.392? Since $0.52 \times 4 = 2.08$ is less than 2.392 and since $0.52 \times 5 = 2.6$ is greater than 2.392, write 4 at the top and write 2.08 below 2.392.

$$\begin{array}{r} 4 \\ 0.52\overline{)2.392} \\ 2.08 \end{array}$$

Subtract 2.08 from 2.392. We get $2.392 - 2.08 = 0.312$. What can we multiply 0.52 by to make 0.312? Since $0.52 \times 0.6 = 0.312$, write a 6 in the tenths place at the top.

$$\begin{array}{r} 4.6 \\ 0.52\overline{)2.392} \\ 2.08 \\ 0.312 \end{array}$$

The answer is $2.392 \div 0.52 = 4.6$. Check the answer by multiplying: $0.52 \times 4.6 = 2.392$.

Exercise Set 5.7

Directions: Divide the numbers.

1) $0.36\overline{)0.2592}$

2) $7.2\overline{)0.1368}$

3) $0.049\overline{)0.392}$

4) $0.83\overline{)0.5312}$

5) $5.4 \overline{)20.79}$

6) $0.018 \overline{)0.954}$

7) $0.91 \overline{)4.277}$

8) $0.0027 \overline{)0.216}$

9) $0.065 \overline{)0.247}$

10) $0.26 \overline{)0.0143}$

11) $8.8 \overline{)0.02024}$

12) $0.052 \overline{)0.4524}$

13) $0.49 \overline{)8.036}$

14) $5.8 \overline{)20.3}$

15) $0.075 \overline{)5.13}$

16) $0.0094 \overline{)0.423}$

5 Divide Decimals

5.8 Whole Number Division with Decimal Quotients

When one whole number is divided by another whole number, it is possible for the answer (called the quotient) to be a decimal. This happens when the numbers do not divide evenly, such that there is a remainder. Instead of writing a remainder, we will write the answer as a decimal. The same strategy that we used to divide numbers in Sec.'s 5.2-5.3 applies to these problems.

Example 1. What is $21 \div 4$?

Write the dividend (21) inside of the long division symbol and the divisor (4) to the left of the long division symbol.

$$4\overline{)21}$$

Since $4 \times 5 = 20$, write 5 at the top and write 20 below 21.

$$\begin{array}{r} 5 \\ 4\overline{)21} \\ 20 \end{array}$$

Add a .0 to the 21 to make 21.0. Subtract 20 from 21.0. We get $21.0 - 20 = 1.0$. Since $4 \times 0.2 = 0.8$, write a 2 in the tenths place at the top and write 0.8 below 1.0.

$$\begin{array}{r} 5.2 \\ 4\overline{)21.0} \\ \underline{20} \\ 1.0 \\ 0.8 \end{array}$$

Add a 0 to the 21.0 to make 21.00. Subtract 0.8 from 1.0. We get $1.0 - 0.8 = 0.20$. Since $4 \times 0.05 = 0.20$, write a 5 in the hundredths place at the top.

$$\begin{array}{r} 5.25 \\ 4\overline{)21.00} \\ \underline{20} \\ 1.0 \\ \underline{0.8} \\ 0.20 \end{array}$$

The answer is $21 \div 4 = 5.25$. Check the answer by multiplying: $4 \times 5.25 = 21$.

Master Decimals Math Practice Workbook with Answers

Example 2. What is $3 \div 4$?

Write the dividend (3) inside of the long division symbol and the divisor (4) to the left of the long division symbol.

$$4\overline{)3}$$

Add a .0 to the 3 to make 3.0. Since $4 \times 0.7 = 2.8$, write 0.7 at the top and write 2.8 below 3.0.

$$\begin{array}{r} 0.7 \\ 4\overline{)3.0} \\ 2.8 \end{array}$$

Add a .0 to the 3.0 to make 3.00. Subtract 2.8 from 3.00. We get $3.00 - 2.8 = 0.20$. Since $4 \times 0.05 = 0.20$, write a 5 in the hundredths place at the top.

$$\begin{array}{r} 0.75 \\ 4\overline{)3.00} \\ \underline{2.8} \\ 0.20 \end{array}$$

The answer is $3 \div 4 = 0.75$. Check the answer by multiplying: $4 \times 0.75 = 3$.

Note: An alternative way to divide whole numbers is to make a fraction and convert the fraction to a decimal (Chapter 6). For example, $3 \div 4$ is equivalent to $\frac{3}{4}$.

Exercise Set 5.8

Directions: Divide the numbers.

1) $5\overline{)43}$

2) $4\overline{)11}$

3) $2\overline{)7}$

4) $8\overline{)3}$

5 Divide Decimals

5) 4)1

6) 8)71

7) 5)4

8) 2)1

9) 5)46

10) 2)15

11) 8)5

12) 4)10

13) 8)1

14) 4)501

15) 8)100

16) 5)2

17) $10\overline{)37}$

18) $25\overline{)40}$

19) $16\overline{)9}$

20) $40\overline{)300}$

21) $20\overline{)4}$

22) $32\overline{)24}$

23) $50\overline{)115}$

24) $25\overline{)1010}$

25) $80\overline{)600}$

26) $16\overline{)11}$

27) $250\overline{)700}$

28) $125\overline{)75}$

5.9 Division Word Problems

The word problems in this section involve dividing decimals (and may also involve addition, subtraction, or multiplication).

Example 1. If it costs $2.73 to buy 7 bananas, how much does each banana cost? Divide $2.73 by 7:

$$\begin{array}{r} 0.39 \\ 7\overline{)2.73} \\ \underline{2.1} \\ 0.63 \end{array}$$

Each banana costs $0.39.

Exercise Set 5.9

Directions: Determine the answer to each word problem.

1) Three friends pay $4.95 for a bag of popcorn. How much should each friend pay in order to split the cost equally? (There is no sales tax.)

2) When one dozen identical blocks are placed on a scale, the scale reads 6.84 ounces. How much does each block weigh?

3) A person hikes 2.4 miles in one-half of an hour. What is the person's average speed in miles per hour?

4) Alice had $108. She spent one-sixth of her money on books. After buying the books, she spent one-fourth of her remaining money on a gift for her mother. After buying her mother a gift, Alice spent one-fifth of her remaining money to watch a movie. How much money did Alice have left after watching the movie?

5) An elevator can support a load of 1500 pounds. There are 8 adults on the elevator; the adults weigh about 145 pounds each. Before the elevator doors close, a group of kids arrive; each kid weighs about 80 pounds. How many kids can ride on the elevator along with the adults?

5.10 Average Values

To find the average of a set of values, add up all of the values and divide by the total number of values in the set. We can express this with the following formula:

$$\bar{x} = \frac{x_1 + x_2 + \cdots + x_N}{N}$$

- $\bar{x}$ (with a bar over it) represents the average value
- $x_1, x_2, \ldots, x_N$ represent the individual values
- N is the total number of values in the set

Example 1. Find the average value of 0.76, 0.8, and 0.87.
There are 3 values. Add the values up and divide by 3:

$$\bar{x} = \frac{0.76 + 0.8 + 0.87}{3} = \frac{2.43}{3} = 2.43 \div 3 = \boxed{0.81}$$

Note: You should stack the numbers 0.76, 0.8, and 0.87 to add them like we added numbers in Chapter 3, and you should write 2.43 ÷ 3 as a long division problem like we did in the earlier sections of this chapter.

Example 2. Find the average value of 1.4, 1.9, 2, and 2.7.
There are 4 values. Add the values up and divide by 4:

$$\bar{x} = \frac{1.4 + 1.9 + 2 + 2.7}{4} = \frac{8}{4} = 8 \div 4 = \boxed{2}$$

Exercise Set 5.10

Directions: Find the average value for each list of numbers.

1) 0.37 and 0.41

2) 5.8, 5.93, and 6

3) 0.074, 0.074, 0.077, 0.077, and 0.077

4) 1.234, 1.423, 1.342

5) 0.764, 0.77, 0.781, 0.8

6) 0.089, 0.09, 0.096, 0.1, 0.103, and 0.11

5 Divide Decimals

5.11 Which Number Is Closer?

Given the numbers 0.043 and 0.051, how can you determine which number is closer to 0.0468? One way is to find the average:

$$\frac{0.043 + 0.051}{2} = \frac{0.094}{2} = 0.047$$

Since 0.0468 is less than the average (0.047), the smaller value (0.043) is closer to 0.0468 than the larger value (0.051). (An alternative method is to find the absolute value of the difference between each number and 0.0468. Since $|0.043 - 0.0468| = |-0.0038| = 0.0038$ is less than $|0.051 - 0.0468| = |0.0042|$, this shows that 0.043 is closer to 0.0468 than 0.051 is. The absolute value of a number means to ignore any minus sign that the number may have.)

It may help to review Chapter 2.

Example 1. Is 0.86 or 0.89 closer to 0.863?
Find the average value:

$$\frac{0.86 + 0.89}{2} = \frac{1.75}{2} = 0.875$$

Since 0.863 is less than the average (8.75), the smaller value (0.86) is closer to 0.863.

Example 2. Is 4.8 or 6.1 closer to 5.47?
Find the average value:

$$\frac{4.8 + 6.1}{2} = \frac{10.9}{2} = 5.45$$

Since 5.47 is greater than the average (5.45), the larger value (6.1) is closer to 5.47.

Example 3. Is 0.0034 or 0.0037 closer to 0.004?
It is not necessary to find the average value to answer this question. Both values are less than 0.004. Since 0.0037 is greater than 0.0034, the value 0.0037 is closer to 0.004.

Example 4. Is 0.57 or 0.61 closer to 0.49?
It is not necessary to find the average value to answer this question. Both values are greater than 0.49. Since 0.57 is less than 0.61, the value 0.57 is closer to 0.49.

Master Decimals Math Practice Workbook with Answers

Exercise Set 5.11

Directions: Determine which of the two values is closer to the specified number.

1) Is 0.22 or 0.255 closer to 0.27?

2) Is 0.078 or 0.133 closer to 0.11?

3) Is 1.47 or 1.74 closer to 1.608?

4) Is 0.88 or 0.9 closer to 0.888?

5) Is 18.136 or 18.2 closer to 18?

5 Divide Decimals

6) Is 0.397 or 0.406 closer to 0.4?

7) Is 0.0016 or 0.0032 closer to 0.00239?

8) Is 6.238 or 6.328 closer to 6.29?

9) Is 0.066 or 0.091 closer to 0.079?

10) Is 0.00373 or 0.0151 closer to 0.00945?

6 FRACTIONS AND DECIMALS

$$\begin{array}{r} 0.875 \\ 8\overline{)7.000} \\ \underline{6.4} \\ 0.60 \\ \underline{0.56} \\ 0.040 \end{array}$$

$$\frac{7}{8} = \frac{7 \times 125}{8 \times 125} = \frac{875}{1000} = 0.875$$

$$0.64 = \frac{64}{100} = \frac{64 \div 4}{100 \div 4} = \frac{16}{25}$$

$$2\frac{3}{4} = 2 + \frac{3}{4} = 2 + \frac{3 \times 25}{4 \times 25} = 2 + \frac{75}{100} = 2 + 0.75 = 2.75$$

$$1.4 = 1 + 0.4 = 1 + \frac{4}{10} = 1 + \frac{4 \div 2}{10 \div 2} = 1 + \frac{2}{5} = 1\frac{2}{5}$$

$$0.594 < \frac{3}{5} < 0.62 < \frac{2}{3} < 0.7$$

6 Fractions and Decimals

6.1 Convert Fractions to Decimals (Long Division)

One way to convert a fraction to a decimal is to perform long division, like we did in Sec. 5.8. Divide the **numerator** (the top number) of the fraction by the **denominator** (the bottom number) of the fraction. The numerator is the dividend; write it inside of the long division symbol. The denominator is the divisor; write it to the left of the long division symbol.

Example 1. Use long division to convert $\frac{5}{4}$ to a decimal.

Divide 5 by 4. Write the numerator (5) inside of the long division symbol. Write the denominator (4) to the left of the long division symbol.

$$\begin{array}{r} 1.25 \\ 4\overline{)5.00} \\ \underline{4} \\ 1.0 \\ \underline{0.8} \\ 0.20 \end{array}$$

Example 2. Use long division to convert $\frac{4}{5}$ to a decimal.

Divide 4 by 5. Write the numerator (4) inside of the long division symbol. Write the denominator (5) to the left of the long division symbol.

$$\begin{array}{r} 0.8 \\ 5\overline{)4.0} \end{array}$$

Note: It is instructive to compare these two examples. In Example 1, $\frac{5}{4} = 1.25$ is larger than 1 because the numerator is larger than the denominator. In Example 2, $\frac{4}{5} = 0.8$ is smaller than 1 because the numerator is smaller than the denominator.

Example 3. Use long division to convert $\frac{3}{20}$ to a decimal.

Divide 3 by 20. Write the numerator (3) inside of the long division symbol. Write the denominator (20) to the left of the long division symbol.

$$\begin{array}{r} 0.15 \\ 20\overline{)3.00} \\ \underline{2.0} \\ 1.00 \end{array}$$

Exercise Set 6.1

Directions: Use long division to convert each fraction to a decimal.

1) $\dfrac{1}{2} =$

2) $\dfrac{6}{5} =$

3) $\dfrac{7}{10} =$

4) $\dfrac{1}{4} =$

5) $\dfrac{14}{5} =$

6) $\dfrac{7}{8} =$

7) $\dfrac{11}{20} =$

8) $\dfrac{6}{25} =$

9) $\dfrac{17}{4} =$

10) $\dfrac{11}{8} =$

11) $\dfrac{17}{50} =$

12) $\dfrac{19}{2} =$

13) $\dfrac{28}{5} =$

14) $\dfrac{31}{4} =$

15) $\dfrac{9}{40} =$

16) $\dfrac{5}{16} =$

6.2 Convert Fractions to Decimals (Multiplication)

It is also possible to convert a fraction to a decimal without using long division:
- What is the smallest power of ten (10, 100, 1000, etc.) that the denominator evenly divides into? For example, the 2 of $\frac{1}{2}$ evenly divides into 10, the 4 of $\frac{3}{4}$ evenly divides into 100, and the 8 of $\frac{9}{8}$ evenly divides into 1000. (Note that 8 does not evenly divide into 100.)
- Multiply both the numerator and the denominator by the factor needed to make an equivalent fraction where the new denominator equals the answer to the previous step. For example, $\frac{1}{2} = \frac{1 \times 5}{2 \times 5} = \frac{5}{10}$, $\frac{3}{4} = \frac{3 \times 25}{4 \times 25} = \frac{75}{100}$, and $\frac{9}{8} = \frac{9 \times 125}{8 \times 125} = \frac{1125}{1000}$.
- Write the numerator as a decimal where the final decimal position matches the denominator. For example, $\frac{5}{10} = 0.5$, $\frac{75}{100} = 0.75$, and $\frac{1125}{1000} = 1.125$. Look at the decimal position of the last digit in each decimal: 0.5 ends in the tenths, 0.75 ends in the hundredths, and 1.125 ends in the thousandths.

Example 1. Use the multiplication method to convert $\frac{2}{5}$ to a decimal.

Since 5 evenly divides into 10 and since $5 \times 2 = 10$, multiply both the numerator and denominator by 2 in order to make an equivalent fraction with a denominator of 10:
$$\frac{2}{5} = \frac{2 \times 2}{5 \times 2} = \frac{4}{10} = \boxed{0.4}$$
Since the denominator is 10, we wrote the numerator (4) as a decimal with the last digit (4) in the tenths place.

Example 2. Use the multiplication method to convert $\frac{9}{4}$ to a decimal.

Since 4 evenly divides into 100 and since $25 \times 4 = 100$, multiply both the numerator and denominator by 25 in order to make an equivalent fraction with a denominator of 100:
$$\frac{9}{4} = \frac{9 \times 25}{4 \times 25} = \frac{225}{100} = \boxed{2.25}$$
Since the denominator is 100, we wrote the numerator (225) as a decimal with the last digit (5) in the hundredths place.

Exercise Set 6.2

Directions: Use the multiplication method to convert each fraction to a decimal.

1) $\dfrac{3}{2} =$

2) $\dfrac{3}{5} =$

3) $\dfrac{7}{4} =$

4) $\dfrac{9}{10} =$

5) $\dfrac{17}{20} =$

6) $\dfrac{11}{25} =$

7) $\dfrac{49}{50} =$

8) $\dfrac{5}{8} =$

9)
$$\frac{6}{5} =$$

10)
$$\frac{4}{125} =$$

11)
$$\frac{63}{100} =$$

12)
$$\frac{9}{40} =$$

13)
$$\frac{3}{8} =$$

14)
$$\frac{21}{4} =$$

15)
$$\frac{41}{250} =$$

16)
$$\frac{16}{25} =$$

17)
$$\frac{5}{16} =$$

6 Fractions and Decimals

6.3 Convert Mixed Numbers to Decimals

A **mixed number** combines a whole number and a **proper fraction** together as a single number. An example of a mixed number is $5\frac{2}{3}$, which means five and two-thirds and is equivalent to $5 + \frac{2}{3}$. The whole number 5 plus the proper fraction $\frac{2}{3}$ is equivalent to the **improper fraction** $\frac{17}{3}$. (A proper fraction like $\frac{2}{3}$ has a numerator that is smaller than the denominator; a proper fraction is less than one. An improper fraction like $\frac{17}{3}$ has a numerator that is larger than the denominator; an improper fraction is greater than one. A mixed number is an alternative way of writing an improper fraction. Although we use the term "improper," note that improper fractions are very common in higher-level math courses; there is no reason to avoid improper fractions.)

To convert a mixed number to a decimal, convert the proper fraction to a decimal using any method (Sec. 6.1 or Sec. 6.2) and then add the whole number to it. For example,

$$2\frac{3}{4} = 2 + \frac{3}{4} = 2 + \frac{3 \times 25}{4 \times 25} = 2 + \frac{75}{100} = 2 + 0.75 = 2.75$$

Example 1. Convert $6\frac{7}{20}$ to a decimal.

$$6\frac{7}{20} = 6 + \frac{7}{20} = 6 + \frac{7 \times 5}{20 \times 5} = 6 + \frac{35}{100} = 6 + 0.35 = 6.35$$

Exercise Set 6.3

Directions: Use any method to convert each mixed number to a decimal.

1) $6\frac{1}{4} =$

2) $3\frac{1}{2} =$

3) $1\dfrac{3}{5} =$

4) $5\dfrac{1}{10} =$

5) $4\dfrac{7}{8} =$

6) $9\dfrac{21}{50} =$

7) $7\dfrac{13}{20} =$

8) $2\dfrac{49}{250} =$

9) $26\dfrac{3}{100} =$

10) $47\dfrac{11}{80} =$

6 Fractions and Decimals

6.4 Convert Decimals to Fractions

To convert a decimal to a fraction, follow these steps:
- Remove the decimal point to make the numerator of the fraction. For example, 1.75 has a numerator of 175.
- The denominator is the power of ten associated with the place value of the final decimal position. For example, 1.75 has its final digit (the 5) in the hundredths place, so its denominator is 100.
- Combine the answers to the first two steps into a fraction. For example, 1.75 makes the fraction $\frac{175}{100}$.
- If the numerator and denominator share a common factor, divide the numerator and denominator each by the greatest common factor in order to reduce the fraction. For example, since 175 and 100 are each evenly divisible by 25, we can reduce $\frac{175}{100}$ as follows: $\frac{175}{100} = \frac{175 \div 25}{100 \div 25} = \frac{7}{4}$.

Example 1. Convert 0.8 to a reduced fraction.

Since the final digit (8) is in the tenths place, the fraction is $\frac{8}{10}$. Since 8 and 10 are each evenly divisible by 2, we can reduce the fraction: $\frac{8}{10} = \frac{8 \div 2}{10 \div 2} = \frac{4}{5}$.

Example 2. Convert 1.24 to a reduced fraction.

Since the final digit (4) is in the hundredths place, the fraction is $\frac{124}{100}$. Since 124 and 100 are each evenly divisible by 4, we can reduce the fraction: $\frac{124}{100} = \frac{124 \div 4}{100 \div 4} = \frac{31}{25}$.

Example 3. Convert 0.072 to a reduced fraction.

Since the final digit (2) is in the thousandths place, the fraction is $\frac{72}{1000}$. Since 72 and 1000 are each evenly divisible by 8, we can reduce the fraction: $\frac{72}{1000} = \frac{72 \div 8}{1000 \div 8} = \frac{9}{125}$.

Exercise Set 6.4

Directions: Convert each decimal to a reduced fraction.

1) $0.5 =$

2) $1.25 =$

3) $0.625 =$

4) $0.4 =$

5) $1.68 =$

6) $0.775 =$

7) $5.5 =$

8) $0.08 =$

9) $1.52 =$

10) $10.1 =$

11) $1.375 =$

12) $2.25 =$

13) $0.2 =$

14) $0.048 =$

15) $0.86 =$

16) $3.2 =$

17) $1.736 =$

18) $0.35 =$

19) $2.5 =$

20) $0.272 =$

6.5 Convert Decimals to Mixed Numbers

If a decimal is greater than one, the decimal may be converted to a mixed number as an alternative to the improper fractions that we made in Sec. 6.4. To convert a decimal that is greater than one to a mixed number, follow these steps:

- Separate the decimal into a whole number plus a decimal part. For example, 3.25 can be separated into 3 plus 0.25.
- Convert the decimal part to a proper fraction using the method from Sec. 6.4. For example, $0.25 = \frac{25}{100} = \frac{25 \div 25}{100 \div 25} = \frac{1}{4}$.
- Combine the whole number from the first step with the proper fraction from the second step to make the mixed number. For example, $3.25 = 3\frac{1}{4}$.

Example 1. Convert 1.6 to a mixed number.

Separate 1.6 into 1 plus 0.6. Convert 0.6 to a proper fraction: $0.6 = \frac{6}{10} = \frac{6 \div 2}{10 \div 2} = \frac{3}{5}$. Put the whole number (1) and the proper fraction $\left(\frac{3}{5}\right)$ together: $1.6 = 1\frac{3}{5}$.

Example 2. Convert 5.24 to a mixed number.

Separate 5.24 into 5 plus 0.24. Convert 0.24 to a proper fraction: $0.24 = \frac{24}{100} = \frac{24 \div 4}{100 \div 4} = \frac{6}{25}$. Put the whole number (5) and the proper fraction $\left(\frac{6}{25}\right)$ together: $5.24 = 5\frac{6}{25}$.

Exercise Set 6.5

Directions: Convert each decimal to a mixed number with a reduced proper fraction.

1) 4.25 =

2) 6.5 =

3) 3.8 =

4) 2.049 =

Master Decimals Math Practice Workbook with Answers

5) 1.5 =

6) 8.75 =

7) 3.125 =

8) 5.2 =

9) 2.4 =

10) 4.066 =

11) 9.25 =

12) 7.16 =

13) 6.1 =

14) 1.6 =

15) 4.375 =

16) 3.92 =

17) 8.54 =

18) 2.136 =

19) 7.8 =

20) 16.45 =

6.6 Word Problems with Fractions and Decimals

The word problems in this section involve fractions and decimals.

Example 1. A student buys a calculator that costs $18.75 in a state where there is no sales tax. The student uses a coupon so that the student only has to pay four-fifths of the price. How much does the student need to pay for the calculator?

First convert four-fifths to a decimal: $\frac{4}{5} = \frac{4 \times 2}{5 \times 2} = \frac{8}{10} = 0.8$. Now multiply $18.75 by 0.8:

$$\begin{array}{r} {\scriptstyle 7\ 6\ 4} \\ \$18.75 \\ \times\ 0.8 \\ \hline \$15.000 \end{array}$$

The student must pay $15 for the calculator.

Exercise Set 6.6

Directions: Determine the answer to each word problem.

1) An animal travels 5.4 miles in three quarters of an hour. What is the average speed of the animal?

2) A rope is initially 3.24 feet long. Seven-tenths of a foot are cut off from one end of the rope and discarded. How long is the section of rope that remains?

3) Dan paid $8.25 for a pizza. Dan's friend, Ben, ate two-fifths of the pizza. Ben pays Dan for the amount of pizza that Ben ate. How much money should Ben pay Dan?

4) If one bag of flour weighs 2.26 kilograms, what is the combined weight of two and three-fifths bags of flour?

5) A movie is 1.6 hours long. After watching the movie for five-eighths of an hour, how much time remains?

6.7 Compare Fractions and Decimals

To compare a fraction to a decimal, convert the fraction to a decimal and then compare the two decimals like we did in Chapter 2.

Example 1. Compare 0.746 to $\frac{3}{4}$.

First convert $\frac{3}{4}$ to a decimal: $\frac{3}{4} = \frac{3 \times 25}{4 \times 25} = \frac{75}{100} = 0.75$. Since $0.746 < 0.75$, it follows that $0.746 < \frac{3}{4}$.

Exercise Set 6.7

Directions: Write $<$, $>$, or $=$ between each pair of numbers.

1) $0.62 \quad \frac{3}{5}$

2) $\frac{5}{2} \quad 2.47$

3) $\frac{13}{4} \quad 3.5$

4) $0.85 \quad \frac{17}{20}$

5) $0.15 \quad \frac{21}{125}$

6) $1.4 \quad \frac{67}{50}$

7) $0.048 \quad \frac{1}{20}$

8) $\frac{7}{8} \quad 0.88$

9) $\frac{3}{16} \quad 0.187$

10) $0.225 \quad \frac{9}{40}$

7 REPEATING DECIMALS

```
    0.333...
3)1.0000
   0.9
   0.10
   0.09
   0.010
   0.009
   0.0010
```

$$\frac{1}{3} = \frac{1 \times 3}{3 \times 3} = \frac{3}{9} = 0.33333333... = 0.\bar{3}$$

```
      0.6363...
11)7.0000
   6.6
   0.40
   0.33
   0.070
   0.066
   0.0040
   0.0033
   0.00070
```

$$\frac{7}{11} = \frac{7 \times 9}{11 \times 9} = \frac{63}{99} = 0.63636363... = 0.\overline{63}$$

```
       1.0666...
15)16.0000
   15
    1.0
    0.0
    1.00
    0.90
    0.100
    0.090
    0.0100
    0.0090
    0.00100
```

$$\frac{16}{15} = 1 + \frac{1}{15} = 1 + \frac{1 \times 6}{15 \times 6} = 1 + \frac{6}{90} = 1 + \frac{1}{10} \times \frac{6}{9}$$
$$= 1 + \frac{1}{10} 0.\bar{6} = 1 + 0.0\bar{6} = 1.06666666... = 1.0\bar{6}$$

7 Repeating Decimals

7.1 Notation for Repeating Decimals

When some fractions are converted to decimals, one or more digits repeat forever, like the examples below for $\frac{1}{3}, \frac{7}{11}$, and $\frac{16}{15}$. These are called **repeating decimals**.

$$
\begin{array}{r}
0.333... \\
3\overline{)1.0000} \\
\underline{0.9} \\
0.10 \\
\underline{0.09} \\
0.010 \\
\underline{0.009} \\
0.0010
\end{array}
\qquad
\begin{array}{r}
0.6363... \\
11\overline{)7.0000} \\
\underline{6.6} \\
0.40 \\
\underline{0.33} \\
0.070 \\
\underline{0.066} \\
0.0040 \\
\underline{0.0033} \\
0.00070
\end{array}
\qquad
\begin{array}{r}
1.0666... \\
15\overline{)16.0000} \\
\underline{15} \\
1.0 \\
\underline{0.0} \\
1.00 \\
\underline{0.90} \\
0.100 \\
\underline{0.090} \\
0.0100 \\
\underline{0.0090} \\
0.00100
\end{array}
$$

In Sec. 7.2, we will use long division to form repeating decimals, like the examples above. In the current section, the focus is on understanding the notation for repeating decimals.

We place a bar over the digits that repeat. For example, $\frac{1}{3} = 0.33333333...$ has a single digit repeating, so just one digit has a bar over it: $\frac{1}{3} = 0.\overline{3}$. The notation $0.\overline{3}$ is a short-hand way of writing 0.33333333... (with the 3 repeating forever). As another example, $\frac{7}{11} = 0.63636363...$ has a pair of digits repeating, so two digits have a bar over them: $\frac{7}{11} = 0.\overline{63}$. The notation $0.\overline{63}$ is a short-hand way of writing 0.63636363... (with the 63 repeating forever).

Sometimes, there are digits that do not repeat in addition to repeating decimals. For example, the number 0.542424242... has a non-repeating 5 in addition to the repeating pair 42. This decimal is written as $0.5\overline{42}$. Look closely: the 42 is under the bar, but the 5 is not. If we put all three digits under the bar, we would get $0.\overline{542} = 0.542542542...$ instead of 0.542424242...

Example 1. $0.\overline{7} = 0.77777777...$ The 7 repeats forever.
Example 2. $0.\overline{82} = 0.82828282...$ The group 82 repeats forever.
Example 3. $0.8\overline{2} = 0.82222222...$ Only the 2 repeats.

Exercise Set 7.1

Directions: Write out the first several digits of each number.

1) $0.\overline{2} =$

2) $0.\overline{49} =$

3) $0.\overline{861} =$

4) $0.5\overline{3} =$

5) $0.24\overline{76} =$

6) $0.\overline{7} =$

7) $0.\overline{03} =$

8) $0.\overline{30} =$

9) $0.0\overline{3} =$

10) $2.\overline{1} =$

11) $0.\overline{655} =$

12) $0.\overline{565} =$

13) $0.\overline{556} =$

14) $0.\overline{009} =$

15) $0.\overline{090} =$

16) $0.\overline{900} =$

17) $5.3\overline{48} =$

18) $0.002\overline{898} =$

19) $1.23\overline{456789} =$

20) $0.\overline{4114} =$

7 Repeating Decimals

Example 4. $0.55555555... = 0.\overline{5}$ The 5 repeats forever.
Example 5. $0.14141414... = 0.\overline{14}$ The group 14 repeats forever.
Example 6. $0.37777777... = 0.3\overline{7}$ Only the 7 repeats.

Directions: Rewrite each number using repeating decimal notation.

21) $0.88888888... =$

22) $5.2525252... =$

23) $0.747274727472... =$

24) $1.99999999... =$

25) $0.428571428571428571... =$

26) $16.32846846846... =$

27) $0.5677777777... =$

28) $0.1867867867867... =$

29) $1.034343434... =$

30) $763.2323232... =$

31) $0.00021212121... =$

32) $3.363363363363... =$

33) $0.336336336336... =$

34) $0.663663663663... =$

35) $0.0022222222... =$

36) $0.010010010010... =$

37) $0.100100100100... =$

38) $8.80880880880... =$

39) $0.0060606060... =$

40) $0.22255555555... =$

7.2 Repeating Decimals from Long Division

During long division, a repeating decimal forms if a group of digits repeats forever.

Example 1. Use long division to convert $\frac{1}{3}$ to a decimal.

Divide the numerator (1) by the denominator (3). Write 1 inside of the long division symbol and write 3 to the left. In the answer, the 3 repeats forever.

$$
\begin{array}{r}
0.333\ldots \\
3\overline{)1.0000} \\
\underline{0.9} \\
0.10 \\
\underline{0.09} \\
0.010 \\
\underline{0.009} \\
0.0010
\end{array}
$$

The final answer is $\frac{1}{3} = 0.\overline{3}$.

Example 2. Use long division to convert $\frac{7}{11}$ to a decimal.

Divide the numerator (7) by the denominator (11). Write 7 inside of the long division symbol and write 11 to the left. In the answer, the group 63 repeats forever.

$$
\begin{array}{r}
0.6363\ldots \\
11\overline{)7.0000} \\
\underline{6.6} \\
0.40 \\
\underline{0.33} \\
0.070 \\
\underline{0.066} \\
0.0040 \\
\underline{0.0033} \\
0.00070
\end{array}
$$

The final answer is $\frac{7}{11} = 0.\overline{63}$.

7 Repeating Decimals

Example 3. Use long division to convert $\frac{16}{15}$ to a decimal.

Divide the numerator (16) by the denominator (15). Write 16 inside of the long division symbol and write 15 to the left. In the answer, the 6 repeats forever.

$$
\begin{array}{r}
1.0666... \\
15{\overline{\smash{\big)}\,16.0000}} \\
\underline{15} \\
1.0 \\
\underline{0.0} \\
1.00 \\
\underline{0.90} \\
0.100 \\
\underline{0.090} \\
0.0100 \\
\underline{0.0090} \\
0.00100
\end{array}
$$

The final answer is $\frac{16}{15} = 1.0\overline{6}$ (only the 6 repeats).

Exercise Set 7.2

Directions: Convert each fraction to a decimal using long division.

1)
$$\frac{4}{9} =$$

2)
$$\frac{2}{3} =$$

3) $\dfrac{8}{11} =$

4) $\dfrac{10}{9} =$

5) $\dfrac{1}{6} =$

6) $\dfrac{5}{12} =$

7) $\dfrac{7}{30} =$

8) $\dfrac{25}{33} =$

9) $\dfrac{55}{12} =$

10) $\dfrac{4}{15} =$

11)
$$\frac{56}{99} =$$

12)
$$\frac{41}{36} =$$

13)
$$\frac{11}{18} =$$

14)
$$\frac{5}{7} =$$

7.3 Which Fractions Form Repeating Decimals?

Some fractions form repeating decimals, like $\frac{2}{3} = 0.\overline{6}$ and $\frac{17}{132} = 0.12\overline{87}$, while other fractions form non-repeating decimals, like $\frac{3}{4} = 0.75$ and $\frac{21}{80} = 0.2625$. Of the fractions that form repeating decimals, some repeat quickly, like $\frac{8}{11} = 0.\overline{72}$, while in other cases it takes several digits to see the repetition, like $\frac{2}{7} = 0.\overline{285714}$ and $\frac{8}{13} = 0.\overline{615384}$.

You can tell whether or not a fraction will form a repeating decimal by looking at the **factors** of the denominator, provided that the fraction is **reduced**: Which numbers evenly divide into the denominator of the reduced form of the fraction?

- If the denominator can be formed exclusively by multiplying 2's and 5's, the decimal will have a finite number of digits. For example, $\frac{21}{80}$ does not form a repeating decimal because 80 can be formed by multiplying $2 \times 2 \times 2 \times 2 \times 5 = 4 \times 4 \times 5 = 16 \times 5 = 80$. As a decimal, $\frac{21}{80} = 0.2625$.
- If the denominator has any **prime** factors other than 2 or 5, the fraction forms a repeating decimal. For example, the number 55 factors as $5 \times 11 = 55$. Since 11 is a prime factor other than 2 and 5, any **reduced** fraction with a denominator of 55 will form a repeating decimal. For example, $\frac{18}{55} = 0.3\overline{27}$.

Example 1. Does the fraction $\frac{71}{250}$ form a repeating decimal?
No. The denominator can be formed by multiplying 2's and 5's together:
$$5 \times 5 \times 5 \times 2 = 250$$
Example 2. Does the fraction $\frac{71}{60}$ form a repeating decimal?
Yes. The fraction $\frac{71}{60}$ is reduced because the numerator and denominator do not share any common factors, and the denominator has a **prime** factor that is different from 2 and 5. The prime factors include a 3:
$$2 \times 2 \times 3 \times 5 = 60$$

Master Decimals Math Practice Workbook with Answers

Example 3. Does the fraction $\frac{12}{30}$ form a repeating decimal?

No. Since the numerator and denominator are each evenly divisible by 6, the fraction $\frac{12}{30}$ can be reduced:

$$\frac{12}{30} = \frac{12 \div 6}{30 \div 6} = \frac{2}{5}$$

The fraction $\frac{2}{5}$ is the reduced form of $\frac{12}{30}$. Look at the reduced form of the fraction to tell if the fraction will form a repeating decimal. The denominator of the reduced fraction equals 5, so it can definitely be formed exclusively from 2's and 5's.

Example 4. Does the fraction $\frac{8}{30}$ form a repeating decimal?

Yes. Since the numerator and denominator are each evenly divisible by 2, the fraction $\frac{8}{30}$ can be reduced:

$$\frac{8}{30} = \frac{8 \div 2}{30 \div 2} = \frac{4}{15}$$

The fraction $\frac{4}{15}$ is the reduced form of $\frac{8}{30}$. The denominator of the reduced fraction, $\frac{4}{15}$, has a **prime** factor that is different from 2 and 5. The prime factors include a 3.

$$3 \times 5 = 15$$

Exercise Set 7.3

Directions: Indicate whether or not each fraction forms a repeating decimal. Explain your answer based on the prime factors of the reduced form of each fraction.

1) Does the fraction $\frac{9}{70}$ form a repeating decimal?

2) Does the fraction $\frac{49}{1250}$ form a repeating decimal?

3) Does the fraction $\frac{63}{550}$ form a repeating decimal?

4) Does the fraction $\frac{11}{65}$ form a repeating decimal?

5) Does the fraction $\frac{13}{65}$ form a repeating decimal?

6) Does the fraction $\frac{99}{250}$ form a repeating decimal?

7) Does the fraction $\frac{25}{70}$ form a repeating decimal?

8) Does the fraction $\frac{28}{70}$ form a repeating decimal?

9) Does the fraction $\frac{189}{63}$ form a repeating decimal?

7.4 Method of Nines (Without Zeros)

It is possible to convert a fraction to a repeating decimal without using long division. We will refer to this as the "method of nines." We will discuss the simplest case in this section, and the two other possible cases in Sec.'s 7.5-7.6.

If the fraction forms a repeating decimal, the numerator is smaller than the denominator, and the denominator evenly divides into a whole number where every digit is a 9 (like 9, 99, 999, or 9999), follow these steps to convert the fraction to a repeating decimal:

- What is the smallest whole number where every digit is a 9 that the denominator evenly divides into? For example, the 3 of $\frac{2}{3}$ evenly divides into 9, the 11 of $\frac{8}{11}$ evenly divides into 99, and the 27 of $\frac{4}{27}$ evenly divides into 999 (since $27 \times 37 = 999$).
- Multiply both the numerator and the denominator by the factor needed to make an equivalent fraction where the new denominator equals the answer to the previous step. For example, $\frac{2}{3} = \frac{2 \times 3}{3 \times 3} = \frac{6}{9}, \frac{8}{11} = \frac{8 \times 9}{11 \times 9} = \frac{72}{99}$, and $\frac{4}{27} = \frac{4 \times 37}{27 \times 37} = \frac{148}{999}$.
- Write the numerator as a repeating decimal where the final decimal position matches the number of 9's in the denominator. For example, $\frac{6}{9} = 0.\overline{6}, \frac{72}{99} = 0.\overline{72}$, and $\frac{148}{999} = 0.\overline{148}$.
- Beware of possible repeating 0's. For example, compare $\frac{7}{99} = 0.\overline{07}$ to $\frac{7}{9} = 0.\overline{7}$ and $\frac{74}{99} = 0.\overline{74}$, compare $\frac{40}{99} = 0.\overline{40}$ to $\frac{41}{99} = 0.\overline{41}$, compare $\frac{2}{999} = 0.\overline{002}$ to $\frac{212}{999} = 0.\overline{212}$, and compare $\frac{50}{999} = 0.\overline{050}$ to $\frac{5}{999} = 0.\overline{005}$ and $\frac{500}{999} = 0.\overline{500}$.

Example 1. $\frac{2}{3} = \frac{2 \times 3}{3 \times 3} = \frac{6}{9} = 0.\overline{6}$

Example 2. $\frac{14}{33} = \frac{14 \times 3}{33 \times 3} = \frac{42}{99} = 0.\overline{42}$

Example 3. $\frac{1}{11} = \frac{1 \times 9}{11 \times 9} = \frac{9}{99} = 0.\overline{09}$

Example 4. $\frac{20}{111} = \frac{20 \times 9}{111 \times 9} = \frac{180}{999} = 0.\overline{180}$

Exercise Set 7.4

Directions: Use the method of nines to convert each fraction to a repeating decimal.

1) $\dfrac{1}{3} =$

2) $\dfrac{2}{9} =$

3) $\dfrac{4}{11} =$

4) $\dfrac{20}{33} =$

5) $\dfrac{14}{333} =$

6) $\dfrac{7}{111} =$

7) $\dfrac{25}{27} =$

8) $\dfrac{512}{3333} =$

9) $\dfrac{36}{101} =$

10) $\dfrac{9}{37} =$

11)
$$\frac{280}{333} =$$

12)
$$\frac{9}{11} =$$

13)
$$\frac{70}{99} =$$

14)
$$\frac{1}{111} =$$

15)
$$\frac{2}{33} =$$

16)
$$\frac{50}{999} =$$

17)
$$\frac{800}{1111} =$$

18)
$$\frac{31}{303} =$$

19)
$$\frac{9}{13} =$$

20)
$$\frac{5}{271} =$$

7.5 Method of Nines (With Zeros)

If the fraction forms a repeating decimal and the numerator is smaller than the denominator, but the denominator does **not** evenly divide into a whole number where every digit is a 9 (like 9, 99, 999, or 9999), follow these steps to convert the fraction to a repeating decimal:

- Although the denominator does not evenly divide into a whole number where every digit is a 9 (like 9, 99, 999, or 9999), it will evenly divide into a whole number that has a series of 9's followed by a series of 0's (like 90, 900, 9000, 990, 9900, or 9990). (Note that all of the 0's must come after the 9's, unlike 909, which has a 0 in between two 9's.)
- What is the smallest whole number with a series of 9's followed by a series of 0's that the denominator evenly divides into? For example, the 15 of $\frac{1}{15}$ evenly divides into 90, the 300 of $\frac{1}{300}$ evenly divides into 900, and the 495 of $\frac{16}{495}$ evenly divides into 990 (since $495 \times 2 = 990$).
- Multiply both the numerator and the denominator by the factor needed to make an equivalent fraction where the new denominator equals the answer to the previous step. For example, $\frac{1}{15} = \frac{1 \times 6}{15 \times 6} = \frac{6}{90}$, $\frac{1}{300} = \frac{1 \times 3}{300 \times 3} = \frac{3}{900}$, and $\frac{16}{495} = \frac{16 \times 2}{495 \times 2} = \frac{32}{990}$.
- Rewrite the fraction as a new fraction that has a denominator with only 9's times a fraction that has a power of 10 as a denominator (like $\frac{1}{10}$ or $\frac{1}{100}$). For example, $\frac{6}{90} = \frac{1}{10} \times \frac{6}{9}$, $\frac{3}{900} = \frac{1}{100} \times \frac{3}{9}$, and $\frac{32}{990} = \frac{1}{10} \times \frac{32}{99}$.
- If the fraction multiplying $\frac{1}{10}$ (or $\frac{1}{100}, \frac{1}{1000}$, etc.) has a numerator that is greater than its denominator (like $\frac{15}{9}$ in $\frac{15}{90} = \frac{1}{10} \times \frac{15}{9}$), you will need to use the strategy of Sec. 7.6 to complete the solution. Otherwise, use the strategy from Sec. 7.4 to rewrite the fraction as a repeating decimal, and use the power of 10 to shift the decimal point (recall Sec. 5.1). For example, $\frac{1}{10} \times \frac{6}{9} = \frac{1}{10} \times 0.\overline{6} = 0.0\overline{6}$, $\frac{1}{100} \times \frac{3}{9} = \frac{1}{100} \times 0.\overline{3} = 0.00\overline{3}$, and $\frac{1}{10} \times \frac{32}{99} = \frac{1}{10} \times 0.\overline{32} = 0.0\overline{32}$.

Master Decimals Math Practice Workbook with Answers

Example 1. $\frac{4}{45} = \frac{4 \times 2}{45 \times 2} = \frac{8}{90} = \frac{1}{10} \times \frac{8}{9} = \frac{1}{10} \times 0.\overline{8} = 0.0\overline{8}$

Example 2. $\frac{1}{150} = \frac{1 \times 6}{150 \times 6} = \frac{6}{900} = \frac{1}{100} \times \frac{6}{9} = \frac{1}{100} \times 0.\overline{6} = 0.00\overline{6}$

Example 3. $\frac{3}{110} = \frac{3 \times 9}{110 \times 9} = \frac{27}{990} = \frac{1}{10} \times \frac{27}{99} = \frac{1}{10} \times 0.\overline{27} = 0.0\overline{27}$

Example 4. $\frac{17}{3300} = \frac{17 \times 3}{3300 \times 3} = \frac{51}{9900} = \frac{1}{100} \times \frac{51}{99} = \frac{1}{100} \times 0.\overline{51} = 0.00\overline{51}$

Exercise Set 7.5

Directions: Use the method of nines to convert each fraction to a repeating decimal.

1) $\frac{1}{30} =$

2) $\frac{1}{4500} =$

3) $\frac{49}{4950} =$

4) $\frac{1}{18} =$

5) $\frac{2}{225} =$

6) $\frac{29}{330} =$

7) $\frac{5}{198} =$

8) $\frac{2}{275} =$

7 Repeating Decimals

9) $\dfrac{83}{99{,}900} =$

10) $\dfrac{2}{45} =$

11) $\dfrac{1}{132} =$

12) $\dfrac{4}{55} =$

13) $\dfrac{3}{1100} =$

14) $\dfrac{124}{4995} =$

15) $\dfrac{1}{1500} =$

16) $\dfrac{5}{66} =$

17) $\dfrac{1}{180} =$

18) $\dfrac{16}{2475} =$

7.6 Method of Nines (Mixed Numbers)

If a fraction forms a repeating decimal and the numerator is larger than the denominator (or when applying the strategy from Sec. 7.5 the new numerator has more digits than the number of 9's in the denominator, like $\frac{15}{90}$ or $\frac{256}{990}$), follow these steps to convert the fraction to a repeating decimal:

- Convert the **improper fraction** to a **mixed number**. Recall that a mixed number is a whole number plus a **proper fraction**. (An improper fraction has a numerator that is larger than its denominator; a proper fraction has a numerator that is smaller than its denominator.) For example, $\frac{8}{3} = 2 + \frac{2}{3}$. The way to do this is to write the numerator as the sum of two numbers, where one of the numbers is the largest multiple of the denominator that is smaller than the numerator. For $\frac{8}{3}$, the largest multiple of 3 that is smaller than 8 is the number 6. Replace 8 with $6 + 2$ to see that $\frac{8}{3} = \frac{6+2}{3} = \frac{6}{3} + \frac{2}{3} = 2 + \frac{2}{3}$.

- Convert the proper fraction to a repeating decimal using the strategy from Sec. 7.4 or 7.5. Add this repeating decimal to the whole number. For example, $\frac{8}{3} = 2 + \frac{2}{3} = 2 + \frac{2 \times 3}{3 \times 3} = 2 + \frac{6}{9} = 2 + 0.\overline{6} = 2.\overline{6}$.

Example 1. $\frac{16}{11} = \frac{11+5}{11} = \frac{11}{11} + \frac{5}{11} = 1 + \frac{5}{11} = 1 + \frac{5 \times 9}{11 \times 9} = 1 + \frac{45}{99} = 1 + 0.\overline{45} = 1.\overline{45}$

Example 2. $\frac{1}{6} = \frac{1 \times 15}{6 \times 15} = \frac{15}{90} = \frac{1}{10} \times \frac{15}{9} = \frac{1}{10} \times \left(\frac{9+6}{9}\right) = \frac{1}{10} \times \left(\frac{9}{9} + \frac{6}{9}\right)$
$= \frac{1}{10} \times \left(1 + \frac{6}{9}\right) = \frac{1}{10} \times (1 + 0.\overline{6}) = \frac{1}{10} \times 1.\overline{6} = 0.1\overline{6}$

Example 3. $\frac{65}{33} = \frac{65 \times 3}{33 \times 3} = \frac{195}{99} = \frac{99+96}{99} = \frac{99}{99} + \frac{96}{99} = 1 + \frac{96}{99} = 1 + 0.\overline{96} = 1.\overline{96}$

Example 4. $\frac{16}{45} = \frac{16 \times 2}{45 \times 2} = \frac{32}{90} = \frac{1}{10} \times \frac{32}{9} = \frac{1}{10} \times \left(\frac{27+5}{9}\right) = \frac{1}{10} \times \left(\frac{27}{9} + \frac{5}{9}\right)$
$= \frac{1}{10} \times \left(3 + \frac{5}{9}\right) = \frac{1}{10} \times (3 + 0.\overline{5}) = \frac{1}{10} \times 3.\overline{5} = 0.3\overline{5}$

Exercise Set 7.6

Directions: Use the method of nines to convert each fraction to a repeating decimal.

1) $\dfrac{4}{3} =$

2) $\dfrac{5}{6} =$

3) $\dfrac{50}{33} =$

4) $\dfrac{85}{9} =$

5) $\dfrac{1}{12} =$

6) $\dfrac{25}{11} =$

7) $\dfrac{11}{30} =$

8) $\dfrac{140}{111} =$

9) $\dfrac{7}{22} =$

10) $\dfrac{2}{15} =$

11) $\dfrac{10}{3} =$

12) $\dfrac{1}{36} =$

13) $\dfrac{7}{225} =$

14) $\dfrac{47}{15} =$

15) $\dfrac{1}{24} =$

16) $\dfrac{9}{55} =$

17) $\dfrac{25}{6} =$

18) $\dfrac{8}{7} =$

19) $\dfrac{3}{275} =$

20) $\dfrac{1}{75} =$

7.7 Convert Repeating Decimals to Fractions

To convert a repeating decimal to a fraction, follow these steps:
- Are there any non-repeating nonzero digits? For example, the 3 in $3.\bar{2}$ is non-repeating whereas the 2 is a repeating decimal. If the number includes non-repeating nonzero digits, rewrite the number as a sum of repeating and non-repeating parts. For example, $3.\bar{2} = 3 + 0.\bar{2}$ and $0.04\overline{36} = 0.04 + 0.00\overline{36}$.
- After the previous step, are there now any zeros between the decimal point and the first repeating digit? For example, $0.00\overline{36}$ has 2 zeros between the 3 and the decimal point. If there are zeros between the decimal point and the first repeating digit, multiply by $\frac{1}{10}, \frac{1}{100}, \frac{1}{1000}$, etc. to shift the decimal point such that there are not any zeros between the decimal point and the first repeating digit (recall Sec. 5.1). For example, $0.00\overline{36} = \frac{1}{100} \times 0.\overline{36}$.
- Write the repeating part as a fraction with the repeating digits in the numerator and the same number of nines in the denominator. For example, $0.\bar{2} = \frac{2}{9}$ and $0.\overline{36} = \frac{36}{99}$.
- If the repeating part multiplied a fraction with a power of ten, multiply these fractions. For example, $\frac{1}{100} \times 0.\overline{36} = \frac{1}{100} \times \frac{36}{99} = \frac{36}{9900}$.
- If the non-repeating part is a decimal, convert it to a fraction (recall Chapter 6). For example, $0.04 = \frac{4}{100}$. (It may be worth waiting until after the next step to reduce the fraction.)
- If the decimal has a non-repeating part, combine the non-repeating part with the fraction from the previous step. For example, $3.\bar{2} = 3 + 0.\bar{2} = 3 + \frac{2}{9} = 3\frac{2}{9}$ and $0.04\overline{36} = 0.04 + 0.00\overline{36} = \frac{4}{100} + \frac{36}{9900}$.
- If two fractions are added together, add them by finding a common denominator. For example, $\frac{4}{100} + \frac{36}{9900} = \frac{4 \times 99}{100 \times 99} + \frac{36}{9900} = \frac{396}{9900} + \frac{36}{9900} = \frac{432}{9900}$.
- If the numerator and denominator share a common factor, reduce the fraction. For example, $\frac{432}{9900} = \frac{432 \div 36}{9900 \div 36} = \frac{12}{275}$.

Example 1. $0.\overline{42} = \frac{42}{99} = \frac{42 \div 3}{99 \div 3} = \frac{14}{33}$

Example 2. $5.\overline{7} = 5 + 0.\overline{7} = 5 + \frac{7}{9} = 5\frac{7}{9}$ or $\frac{5 \times 9 + 7}{9} = \frac{45+7}{9} = \frac{52}{9}$ Note that $\frac{52}{9} = 5\frac{7}{9}$.

Example 3. $0.00\overline{216} = \frac{1}{100} \times 0.\overline{216} = \frac{1}{100} \times \frac{216}{999} = \frac{216}{99,900} = \frac{216 \div 108}{99,900 \div 108} = \frac{2}{925}$

Example 4. $0.3\overline{6} = 0.3 + 0.0\overline{6} = \frac{3}{10} + \frac{1}{10} \times 0.\overline{6} = \frac{3}{10} + \frac{1}{10} \times \frac{6}{9}$
$= \frac{3}{10} + \frac{6}{90} = \frac{3 \times 9}{10 \times 9} + \frac{6}{90} = \frac{27}{90} + \frac{6}{90} = \frac{33}{90} = \frac{33 \div 3}{90 \div 3} = \frac{11}{30}$

Exercise Set 7.7

Directions: Convert each repeating decimal to a reduced fraction.

1) $2.\overline{63} =$

2) $0.\overline{56} =$

3) $0.5\overline{6} =$

4) $0.0\overline{48} =$

5) $0.04\overline{8} =$

6) $0.\overline{048} =$

7) $1.0\overline{7} =$

8) $0.00\overline{96} =$

7 Repeating Decimals

9) $0.\overline{612} =$

10) $2.\overline{50} =$

11) $0.000\overline{72} =$

12) $0.03\overline{8} =$

13) $4.\overline{225} =$

14) $0.36\overline{1} =$

15) $1.\overline{45} =$

16) $0.009\overline{3} =$

17) $0.11\overline{36} =$

18) $1.291\overline{6} =$

19) $0.21\overline{3} =$

20) $0.\overline{761904} =$

8 PERCENTS AND DECIMALS

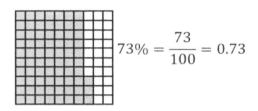

$73\% = \dfrac{73}{100} = 0.73$

36% of $27 = 0.36 \times 27 = 9.72$

$$
\begin{array}{r}
\overset{\scriptscriptstyle 2}{}\\[-2pt]
\overset{\scriptscriptstyle 4}{27}\\
\times\, 0.36\\
\hline
1.62\\
8.10\\
\hline
9.72
\end{array}
$$

$\$45 - 20\%$ of $\$45 = \$45 - 0.2 \times \$45 = \$45 - \$9 = \$36$
$0.8 \times \$45 = \$36$

8.1 Convert Percents to Decimals

A **percent** is a fraction of one hundred. For example, 63% means 63 out of 100, which can also be expressed as $\frac{63}{100}$. Note that we use the word "percent" to refer to a specific numerical value (such as 63%), but use the word "percentage" when the exact value is not stated (such as "a percentage of the students").

To convert a percent to a decimal, divide by 100. It may help to review Sec. 5.1. For example, $63\% = 63 \div 100 = 0.63$.

Example 1. $27\% = 27 \div 100 = 0.27$ (shift the decimal point 2 places to the left)
Example 2. $4.9\% = 4.9 \div 100 = 0.049$ (shift the decimal point 2 places to the left)
Example 3. $140\% = 140 \div 100 = 1.40 = 1.4$ (shift the decimal point 2 places to the left and remove the trailing zero)

Exercise Set 8.1

Directions: Convert each percent to a decimal.

1) 25% =

2) 0.6% =

3) 3.79% =

4) 130% =

5) 80% =

6) 0.04% =

7) 0.865% =

8) 16.3% =

9) 400% =

10) 6.2% =

11) 0.028% =

12) 0.1257% =

13) 57.36% =

14) 0.009% =

15) 0.34% =

16) 216% =

17) 156.27% =

18) 0.0871% =

19) 2.626% =

20) 0.0001% =

8.2 Convert Decimals to Percents

To convert a decimal to a percent, multiply by 100. It may help to review Sec. 4.1. For example, $0.39 = 0.39 \times 100 = 39\%$.

Example 1. $0.71 = 0.71 \times 100\% = 71\%$ (shift the decimal point 2 places to the right)
Example 2. $0.026 = 0.026 \times 100\% = 2.6\%$ (shift the decimal point 2 places to the right)
Example 3. $3.5 = 3.5 \times 100\% = 350\%$ (shift the decimal point 2 places to the right)

Exercise Set 8.2

Directions: Convert each decimal to a percent.

1) $1.2 =$

2) $0.091 =$

3) $0.8 =$

4) $0.0001 =$

5) $0.007 =$

6) $8.842 =$

7) $0.364 =$

8) $0.0025 =$

9) $4 =$

10) $0.109 =$

11) $0.0563 =$

12) $0.00006 =$

13) $0.00979 =$

14) $0.45 =$

8.3 Percent of a Number

To find the percent of a given number, first convert the percent to a decimal and then multiply the numbers using a method from Chapter 4. For example, to find 60% of $7, first divide 60 by 100 to convert 60% to a decimal: $60\% = 60 \div 100 = 0.60 = 0.6$. Now multiply: $0.6 \times \$7 = \$4.20$.

Example 1. What is 80% of 6?
$$80\% = 80 \div 100 = 0.80 = 0.8$$
$$0.8 \times 6 = 4.8$$

Example 2. What is 7% of 14?
$$7\% = 7 \div 100 = 0.07$$

$$\begin{array}{r} \overset{2}{}14 \\ \times\ 0.07 \\ \hline 0.98 \end{array}$$

Example 3. What is 36% of 27?
$$36\% = 36 \div 100 = 0.36$$

$$\begin{array}{r} \overset{2}{\underset{}{\overset{4}{}}}27 \\ \times\ 0.36 \\ \hline 1.62 \\ 8.10 \\ \hline 9.72 \end{array}$$

Exercise Set 8.3

Directions: Determine the indicated percent of each value.

1) What is 50% of 9?

2) What is 4% of 8?

3) What is 0.2% of 3?

4) What is 300% of 6?

8 Percents and Decimals

5) What is 75% of 4?

6) What is 8% of 12?

7) What is 0.63% of 4?

8) What is 0.025% of 7?

9) What is 5.4% of 9?

10) What is 0.3% of 22?

11) What is 48% of 16?

12) What is 3.7% of 6.1?

13) What is 120% of 87?

14) What is 0.68% of 9.2?

15) What is 4.9% of 0.55?

16) What is 74% of 239?

8.4 Percent Increase or Decrease

If a value increases or decreases by a specified percent, there are two ways to find the new value:
- One way is to find the amount of change and then add or subtract the amount of change to the original amount. For example, if $16 is increased by 25%, the amount of change is $16 × 0.25 = $4 and the new amount is $16 + $4 = $20.
- Another way is to add or subtract the percent to 100% and apply the adjusted percent to the original amount. For example, if $16 is increased by 25%, the adjusted percent is 100% + 25% = 125% and the new amount is $16 × 1.25 = $20.

If you know the initial and final values, follow these steps to find the **percent change**:
- First subtract the smaller value from the greater value to determine the amount of change. For example, if $15 decreases to $12, the amount of change equals $15 − $12 = $3.
- Divide the amount of change by the original amount and convert this value to a percent in order to find the percent change. For example, if $15 decreases to $12, the percent change is $3 ÷ $15 = 0.2 = 20%. (Recall from Chapter 5 how to divide decimals.)

Example 1. 18 increases by 40%. Find the new value.
Method 1: 18 × 0.4 = 7.2 such that 18 + 7.2 = 25.2
Method 2: 100% + 40% = 140% such that 18 × 1.4 = 25.2

Example 2. 6.3 decreases by 8%. Find the new value.
Method 1: 6.3 × 0.08 = 0.504 such that 6.3 − 0.504 = 5.796
Method 2: 100% − 8% = 92% such that 6.3 × 0.92 = 5.796

Example 3. 24 increases to 26.4. Find the percent change.
$$\frac{26.4 - 24}{24} = \frac{2.4}{24} = 2.4 \div 24 = 0.1 = 10\%$$ (this is a 10% increase)

Example 4. 7.5 decreases to 6. Find the percent change.
$$\frac{7.5 - 6}{7.5} = \frac{1.5}{7.5} = 1.5 \div 7.5 = 0.2 = 20\%$$ (this is a 20% decrease)

8 Percents and Decimals

Exercise Set 8.4

Directions: Find the indicated value.

1) 60 increases by 15%. Find the new value.

2) 12 decreases by 70%. Find the new value.

3) 36 increases to 45. Find the percent change.

4) 7.2 decreases to 1.8. Find the percent change.

5) 4.2 decreases by 5%. Find the new value.

6) 316 increases to 474. Find the percent change.

7) 0.85 increases by 60%. Find the new value.

8) 0.068 decreases to 0.0442. Find the percent change.

8.5 Word Problems with Percents

The word problems in this section involve percents.

Example 1. A book costs $15. The sales tax is 8%. What is the total cost of the book?
The amount of tax is $15 × 0.08 = $1.2. The total cost is $15 + $1.2 = $16.20.
Example 2. A radio costs $32. A customer has a coupon for 20% off. What is the cost of the radio before adding sales tax?
The amount of the discount is $32 × 0.2 = $6.4. The cost before tax is $32 − $6.4 = $25.60.

Exercise Set 8.5

Directions: Determine the answer to each word problem.

1) A bowl of soup costs $3.60. There is a sales tax of 7.5%. What is the total cost of the soup?

2) The regular price of a television is $795. The television is on sale for 15% off in a state where there is no sales tax. What is the total cost of the television?

3) A suit costs $140. A customer has a coupon for 30% off. There is a sales tax of 10%. What is the total cost of the suit?

4) In a class, 15 out of 20 students are wearing jackets. What percent of the students are wearing jackets?

5) A monkey had 25 bananas. The monkey ate 16% of his bananas. How many bananas remain?

8.6 Compare Fractions, Decimals, and Percents

To compare fractions, decimals, and percents to one another, convert each number to the same form. For example, express every number as a decimal.

Example 1. Compare 0.6 to 63%.
Since 63% = 0.63, it follows that 0.6 < 63%.
Example 2. Compare 38% to $\frac{2}{5}$.
Since 38% = 0.38 and since $\frac{2}{5} = \frac{2\times 2}{5\times 2} = \frac{4}{10} = 0.4$, it follows that 38% < $\frac{2}{5}$.

Exercise Set 8.6

Directions: Write <, >, or = between each pair of numbers.

1) 0.032   4.9%

2) $\frac{3}{4}$ 80%

3) $\frac{8}{5}$ 150%

4) 4.2   78%

5) 0.3%   0.02

6) $\frac{2}{3}$ 70%

8 Percents and Decimals

7) 325% $\frac{7}{2}$

8) 64%   0.6

9) 240%   3.1

10) 63% $\frac{5}{8}$

11) 0.037   0.51%

12) $\frac{8}{11}$ 72%

13) $\frac{9}{20}$ 45%

14) 0.12   8.4%

15) 28%   0.02

16) 116% $\frac{7}{6}$

9 ESTIMATE WITH DECIMALS

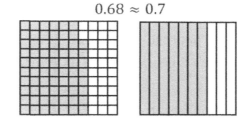

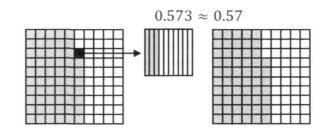

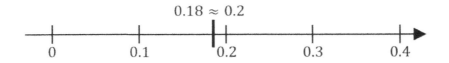

9 Estimate with Decimals

9.1 Round Decimals

Follow these steps to round a decimal:
- Look at the digit that is one place to the right of where you are rounding. For example, to round 6.38 to the nearest tenth, look at the 8 in the hundredths place. To round 0.754 to the nearest hundredth, look at the 4 in the thousandths place.
- If the digit in the previous step is 5 or higher, the digit to its left rounds up. If the digit in the previous step is 4 or lower, the digit to its left rounds down. For example, when 6.38 is rounded to the nearest tenth, the 8 in the hundredths place turns the 3 into a 4 so that 6.38 becomes 6.4. When 0.754 is rounded to the nearest hundredth, the 4 in the thousandths place leaves the 5 unchanged so that 0.754 becomes 0.75. (Note that the digits to the right of the place where you are rounding are removed.)

Example 1. Round 23.619 to the nearest unit.
The 3 is in the units place and the 6 is one digit to its right. Since 6 is 5 or higher, the 3 turns into a 4. The answer is 24.

Example 2. Round 8.729 to the nearest tenth.
The 7 is in the tenths place and the 2 is one digit to its right. Since 2 is 4 or lower, the 7 remains the same. The answer is 8.7.

Example 3. Round 0.4653 to the nearest hundredth.
The 6 is in the hundredths place and the 5 is one digit to its right. Since 5 is 5 or higher, the 6 turns into a 7. The answer is 0.47.

Exercise Set 9.1

Directions: Round each number to the indicated place value.

1) Round 1.674 to the nearest tenth.

2) Round 0.5839 to the nearest hundredth.

3) Round 42.48 to the nearest tenth.

4) Round 0.054 to the nearest hundredth.

5) Round 74.61 to the nearest unit.

6) Round 0.45 to the nearest tenth.

7) Round 0.0882 to the nearest thousandth.

8) Round 0.108 to the nearest hundredth.

9) Round 724.53 to the nearest unit.

10) Round 0.53492 to the nearest thousandth.

11) Round 77.846 to the nearest tenth.

12) Round 2.9357 to the nearest hundredth.

13) Round 86.468 to the nearest unit.

14) Round 0.00191 to the nearest thousandth.

15) Round 7.5 to the nearest unit.

16) Round 0.0094 to the nearest hundredth.

17) Round 9.949 to the nearest tenth.

18) Round 0.6321 to the nearest unit.

19) Round 0.45454 to the nearest thousandth.

20) Round 0.084 to the nearest tenth.

9.2 Round Nines Up

The problems in this section have a 9 in the place value where the number is being rounded, and the number to its right is 5 or higher, causing the 9 to round up.

Example 1. Round 0.096 to the nearest hundredth.
The 9 is in the hundredths place and the 6 is one digit to its right. Since 6 is 5 or higher, the 9 turns into a 10. The answer is 0.10 (which is equivalent to 0.1).

Example 2. Round 3.97 to the nearest tenth.
The 9 is in the tenths place and the 7 is one digit to its right. Since 7 is 5 or higher, the 9 rounds up. When the 9 rounds up, it turns 3.9 into 4.0. The answer is 4.0 (which is equivalent to 4).

Exercise Set 9.2

Directions: Round each number to the indicated place value.

1) Round 0.95 to the nearest tenth.

2) Round 2.999 to the nearest hundredth.

3) Round 49.7 to the nearest unit.

4) Round 0.198 to the nearest hundredth.

5) Round 7.96 to the nearest tenth.

6) Round 0.00595 to the nearest ten thousandth.

7) Round 119.9966 to the nearest hundredth.

8) Round 0.08998 to the nearest ten thousandth.

9) Round 0.09957 to the nearest thousandth.

9.3 Estimate Decimal Addition

One way to estimate the sum of two numbers is to round each number to the same place value. For example, $0.483 + 0.314 \approx 0.5 + 0.3 = 0.8$ to the nearest tenth. (The symbol $\approx$ means "is approximately equal to.")

Example 1. Estimate $5.92 + 0.863$ to the nearest unit.
$$5.92 + 0.863 \approx 6 + 1 = 7$$
Example 2. Estimate $0.632 + 0.284$ to the nearest hundredth.
$$0.632 + 0.284 \approx 0.63 + 0.28 = 0.91$$

Exercise Set 9.3

Directions: Estimate each sum to the indicated place value.

1) Estimate $0.82 + 0.67$ to the nearest tenth.

2) Estimate $6.27 + 1.74$ to the nearest unit.

3) Estimate $0.7652 + 0.4348$ to the nearest hundredth.

4) Estimate $6.83 + 4.18$ to the nearest tenth.

5) Estimate $0.00876 + 0.006482$ to the nearest thousandth.

6) Estimate $36.2 + 19.6$ to the nearest unit.

7) Estimate $2.46 + 0.085$ to the nearest tenth.

8) Estimate $0.49983 + 0.02971$ to the nearest thousandth.

9) Estimate $0.098 + 0.0089$ to the nearest hundredth.

10) Estimate $42.54 + 29.96$ to the nearest tenth.

9.4 Estimate Decimal Subtraction

One way to estimate the difference of two numbers is to round each number to the same place value. For example, $0.872 - 0.566 \approx 0.87 - 0.57 = 0.30 = 0.3$ to the nearest hundredth.

Example 1. Estimate $2.28 - 0.53$ to the nearest tenth.
$$2.28 - 0.53 \approx 2.3 - 0.5 = 1.8$$
Example 2. Estimate $0.471 - 0.159$ to the nearest hundredth.
$$0.471 - 0.159 \approx 0.47 - 0.16 = 0.31$$

Exercise Set 9.4

Directions: Estimate each difference to the indicated place value.

1) Estimate $12.17 - 4.83$ to the nearest tenth.

2) Estimate $1.437 - 0.5544$ to the nearest hundredth.

3) Estimate $26.25 - 8.61$ to the nearest unit.

4) Estimate $0.0632 - 0.00909$ to the nearest hundredth.

5) Estimate $0.0077 - 0.0024$ to the nearest thousandth.

6) Estimate $0.903 - 0.2814$ to the nearest tenth.

7) Estimate $0.746 - 0.381$ to the nearest hundredth.

8) Estimate $19.62 - 7.58$ to the nearest unit.

9) Estimate $0.997 - 0.599$ to the nearest hundredth.

10) Estimate $0.238 - 0.0755$ to the nearest thousandth.

9.5 Estimate Decimal Multiplication

A simple way to estimate the product of two numbers is to round each number to one nonzero digit. (If you keep more digits, you can get a more precise estimate, but the calculation will involve more work.) For example, if we round each number to one nonzero digit, $0.493 \times 0.0627 \approx 0.5 \times 0.06 = 0.030 = 0.03$.

Example 1. Estimate 3.21×0.684.
$$3.21 \times 0.684 \approx 3 \times 0.7 = 2.1$$
Example 2. Estimate 0.403×0.049.
$$0.403 \times 0.049 \approx 0.4 \times 0.05 = 0.020 = 0.02$$

Exercise Set 9.5

Directions: Estimate each product.

1) Estimate 7.89×3.12.

2) Estimate 6.42×0.571.

3) Estimate 0.914×0.809.

4) Estimate 28.4×3.9.

5) Estimate 0.0441×0.0763.

6) Estimate 1.989×0.39.

7) Estimate 0.28×0.041.

8) Estimate 0.055×0.00147.

9) Estimate 7.07×0.0049.

10) Estimate 0.0038×0.00021.

9.6 Estimate Decimal Division

One way to estimate decimal division is to find a division fact (in decimal form) that approximates the problem. For example, $0.331 \div 0.0792$ may be approximated as $0.32 \div 0.08$, for which $0.32 \div 0.08 = 4$. (We are **not** rounding; see the note below.)

Example 1. Estimate $1.58 \div 0.397$.
$$1.58 \div 0.397 \approx 1.6 \div 0.4 = 4$$
Example 2. Estimate $0.247 \div 0.798$.
$$0.247 \div 0.798 \approx 0.24 \div 0.8 = 0.3$$
Note: This is **not** the same as rounding (which is why 0.247 did not become 0.25). Rather, we are looking for a **division fact** (in this case $0.24 \div 0.8$) that is a close approximation.

Exercise Set 9.6

Directions: Estimate each answer.

1) Estimate $2.69 \div 0.318$.

2) Estimate $0.147 \div 0.308$.

3) Estimate $2.82 \div 0.069$.

4) Estimate $0.043 \div 0.689$.

5) Estimate $0.612 \div 0.0019$.

6) Estimate $0.0338 \div 4.84$.

7) Estimate $1.598 \div 0.797$.

8) Estimate $0.0063 \div 0.079$.

9) Estimate $4.398 \div 0.00496$.

10) Estimate $0.00096 \div 9.984$.

ANSWER KEY

Chapter 1 Decimal Place Values

Exercise Set 1.1

1) $0.7 = \frac{7}{10}$

2) $0.61 = \frac{61}{100}$

3) $0.819 = \frac{819}{1000}$

4) $0.5 = \frac{5}{10}$

Note: $\frac{5}{10}$ reduces to $\frac{1}{2}$, but in this section, it is not necessary to reduce your answer. We will reduce answers in Chapter 6.

5) $0.24 = \frac{24}{100}$

6) $0.017 = \frac{17}{1000}$

7) $8.1 = \frac{81}{10}$

8) $0.376 = \frac{376}{1000}$

Note: If there are nonzero digits to the left of the decimal point, like the 8 in 8.1 or like the 15 in 15.2, the fraction will be an improper fraction (meaning that its numerator will be larger than its denominator). Even though we use the word "improper," such fractions are common. There is no reason to avoid them. (You could express them as mixed numbers, but there is no reason to do so. For example, $\frac{81}{10}$ is equivalent to $8\frac{1}{10}$.)

9) $0.09 = \frac{9}{100}$

10) $15.2 = \frac{152}{10}$

11) $1.63 = \frac{163}{100}$

12) $0.0001 = \frac{1}{10,000}$

13) $0.543 = \frac{543}{1000}$

14) $2.5 = \frac{25}{10}$

15) $0.36 = \frac{36}{100}$

16) $0.003 = \frac{3}{1000}$

17) $17.54 = \frac{1754}{100}$

18) $0.6 = \frac{6}{10}$

19) $1.001 = \frac{1001}{1000}$

20) $0.0505 = \frac{505}{10,000}$

Answer Key

Exercise Set 1.2

1) 3.5 =

thousands	hundreds	tens	units	.	tenths	hundredths	thousandths
			3	.	5		

2) 6.792 =

thousands	hundreds	tens	units	.	tenths	hundredths	thousandths
			6	.	7	9	2

3) 42.15 =

thousands	hundreds	tens	units	.	tenths	hundredths	thousandths
		4	2	.	1	5	

4) 0.089 =

thousands	hundreds	tens	units	.	tenths	hundredths	thousandths
			0	.	0	8	9

5) 653.02 =

thousands	hundreds	tens	units	.	tenths	hundredths	thousandths
	6	5	3	.	0	2	

6) 4.634 =

thousands	hundreds	tens	units	.	tenths	hundredths	thousandths
			4	.	6	3	4

7) 5726.3 =

thousands	hundreds	tens	units	.	tenths	hundredths	thousandths
5	7	2	6	.	3		

8) 2415.987 =

thousands	hundreds	tens	units	.	tenths	hundredths	thousandths
2	4	1	5	.	9	8	7

Exercise Set 1.3

1) $65.2 = 60 + 5 + \frac{2}{10}$

2) $1.49 = 1 + \frac{4}{10} + \frac{9}{100}$

3) $0.0083 = \frac{0}{10} + \frac{0}{100} + \frac{8}{1000} + \frac{3}{10,000}$ which simplifies to $\frac{8}{1000} + \frac{3}{10,000}$

4) $729.165 = 700 + 20 + 9 + \frac{1}{10} + \frac{6}{100} + \frac{5}{1000}$

5) $0.4803 = \frac{4}{10} + \frac{8}{100} + \frac{0}{1000} + \frac{3}{10,000}$ which simplifies to $\frac{4}{10} + \frac{8}{100} + \frac{3}{10,000}$

6) $9047.1032 = 9000 + 0 + 40 + 7 + \frac{1}{10} + \frac{0}{100} + \frac{3}{1000} + \frac{2}{10,000}$ which simplifies to $9000 + 40 + 7 + \frac{1}{10} + \frac{3}{1000} + \frac{2}{10,000}$

Exercise Set 1.4

1) $4.63 = 4 + 0.6 + 0.03$
2) $38.2 = 30 + 8 + 0.2$
3) $4.657 = 4 + 0.6 + 0.05 + 0.007$
4) $8256.4 = 8000 + 200 + 50 + 6 + 0.4$
5) $0.00971 = 0.009 + 0.0007 + 0.00001$
6) $42.105 = 40 + 2 + 0.1 + 0.00 + 0.005$ which simplifies to $40 + 2 + 0.1 + 0.005$
7) $70.4902 = 70 + 0 + 0.4 + 0.09 + 0.000 + 0.0002$ which simplifies to $70 + 0.4 + 0.09 + 0.0002$
8) $808.0303 = 800 + 0 + 8 + 0.0 + 0.03 + 0.000 + 0.0003$ which simplifies to $800 + 8 + 0.03 + 0.0003$

Exercise Set 1.5

1) $4.7 =$ four and seven tenths
2) $31.85 =$ thirty-one and eighty-five hundredths
3) $76.573 =$ seventy-six and five hundred seventy-three thousandths
4) $390.19 =$ three hundred ninety and nineteen hundredths
5) $7.07 =$ seven and seven hundredths
6) $456,192.8 =$ four hundred fifty-six thousand, one hundred ninety-two and eight tenths
7) $0.0027 =$ twenty-seven ten thousandths
8) $84.716 =$ eight-four and seven hundred sixteen thousandths

Answer Key

9) 0.000001 = one millionth (When the word is "one," this is the one time where it would not make sense to include the letter "s" at the end of the "th." The word "one" is singular, not plural.)

Note: 0.1 = one tenth, 0.01 = one hundredth, 0.001 = one thousandth, 0.0001 = one ten thousandth, 0.00001 = one hundred thousandth, which is why 0.000001 = one millionth

10) 3.08621 = three and eight thousand six hundred twenty-one hundred thousandths

Note: In Chapter 6, we'll learn that 3.08621 is equivalent to $3 + \frac{8621}{100,000}$.

Exercise Set 1.6

1) the 6 in 2.016 is in the thousandths place
2) the 5 in 35.12 is in the units place (or the ones place)
3) the 2 in 0.527 is in the hundredths place
4) the 4 in 6.48 is in the tenths place
5) the 9 in 94.73 is in the tens place
6) the 1 in 0.015 is in the hundredths place
7) the 8 in 384.6 is in the tens place
8) the 3 in 4.023 is in the thousandths place
9) the 0 in 16.09 is in the tenths place
10) the 7 in 27,456.8 is in the thousands place
11) the 4 in 0.03742 is in the **ten thousandths** place
12) the 6 in 54,328.961 is in the hundredths place
13) the 9 in 6.304189 is in the **millionths** place

Note: The 3 is in the tenths, the 0 is in the hundredths, the 4 is in the thousandths, the 1 is in the ten thousandths, and the 8 is in the hundred thousandths.

14) the 1 in 0.00146 is in the thousandths place
15) the 5 in 3.28375 is in the **hundred thousandths** place

Master Decimals Math Practice Workbook with Answers

Exercise Set 1.7

1) 0.3 =

2) 0.73 =

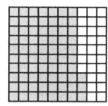

3) 0.487 =

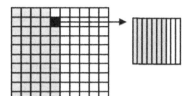

4) 0.9 =

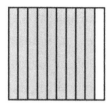

5) 0.25 =

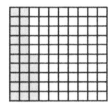

6) 0.068 =

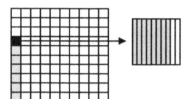

Exercise Set 1.8

1) 0.3, 1.1, 1.5, 2.2

2) 0.07, 0.25, 0.32, 0.46

3) 0.004, 0.019, 0.021, 0.028

Chapter 2 Compare Decimals

Exercise Set 2.1

1) 0.6 has one leading zero (and no trailing zeros) and is equivalent to .6
2) 7.200 has two trailing zeros (both are decimals) and is equivalent to 7.2
3) 0.008 has three leading zeros (two are decimals) and is equivalent to .008
4) 20.00 has three trailing zeros (two are decimals) and is equivalent to 20
5) 0.010 has two leading zeros and one trailing zero, and is equivalent to 0.01 and .01

Note: We offered two equivalent forms in our answers to Problems 5, 8, and 9 just for reference. One equivalent form would be sufficient to answer these questions.

6) 600,010.0 has two trailing zeros (one is a decimal) and is equivalent to 600,010

Notes: There would have been more trailing zeros if the 1 had been a zero. (Compare with Problem 10.) Since the number begins with 6, there are not any leading zeros.

7) 5.00000 has five trailing zeros (all are decimals) and is equivalent to 5

Note: 5 is a whole number. It does not need a decimal point.

8) 0.0037600 has three leading zeros and two trailing zeros, and is equivalent to 0.00376 and .00376
9) 0.04440000 has two leading zeros and four trailing zeros, and is equivalent to 0.0444 and .0444
10) 40,000.0 has five trailing zeros (one is a decimal) and is equivalent to 40,000

Exercise Set 2.2

1) $0.5 < 0.6$ (both are tenths)
2) $0.3 > 0.04$ (tenths > hundredths)
3) $0.2 = 0.20$ (Sec. 2.1: trailing decimal zeros do not affect the value of a number)
4) $0.08 > 0.07$ (both are hundredths)
5) $0.08 > 0.009$ (hundredths > thousandths)
6) $0.6 < 0.7$ (both are tenths)
7) $0.9 < 1$ (tenths < units)
8) $0.0300 = 0.030$ (Sec. 2.1: trailing decimal zeros do not affect the value)

9) 0.004 > 0.003 (both are thousandths)
10) 0.0005 < 0.004 (ten thousandths < thousandths)
11) 4.2 > 3.7 (both leading nonzero digits are units: 4 > 3)
12) 0.58 < 0.7 (both leading nonzero digits are tenths: 0.5 < 0.7)
13) 0.27 > 0.072 (look at the leading nonzero digits: tenths > hundredths)
14) 0.081 > 0.018 (both leading nonzero digits are hundredths: 0.08 > 0.01)
15) 0.6 > 0.094 (look at the leading nonzero digits: tenths > hundredths)
16) 0.0029 < 0.0031 (both leading nonzero digits are thousandths: 0.002 < 0.003)
17) 0.055 < 0.06 (both leading nonzero digits are hundredths: 0.05 < 0.06)
18) 2.1 > 1.975 (both leading nonzero digits are units: 2 > 1)
19) 0.088 < 0.09 (both leading nonzero digits are hundredths: 0.08 < 0.09)
20) 0.0999 < 0.1 (look at the leading nonzero digits: hundredths < tenths)

Exercise Set 2.3

1) 0.85 < 0.87
2) 0.033 > 0.032
3) 2.6 > 2.5
4) 0.0098 < 0.0099
5) 0.073 > 0.07 (since 0.07 = 0.070 and 0.073 > 0.070)
6) 0.4 = 0.40 (Sec. 2.1)
7) 0.5 > 0.058 (look at the place value: tenths > hundredths)
8) 0.006 < 0.0061 (since 0.006 = 0.0060 and 0.0060 < 0.0061)
9) 0.127 < 0.14 (since 0.12 < 0.14)
10) 0.0027 > 0.00028 (look at the place value: thousandths > ten thousandths)
11) 8.3 > 8 (since 8 = 8.0 and 8.3 > 8.0)
12) 0.0911 > 0.09 (since 0.09 = 0.090 and 0.091 > 0.090)

Exercise Set 2.4

1) 0.493 < 0.494
2) 2.36 > 2.354 (since 2.36 > 2.35)

Answer Key

3) $0.0555 > 0.055$ (since $0.055 = 0.0550$ and $0.0555 > 0.0550$)
4) $0.77 = 0.770$ (Sec. 2.1)
5) $0.02478 < 0.247$ (look at the place value: hundredths < tenths)
6) $61.4 > 61$ (since $61 = 61.0$ and $61.4 > 61.0$)
7) $1.787 < 1.792$ (since $1.78 < 1.79$)
8) $0.924 < 0.942$ (since $0.92 < 0.94$; only the first nonzero leading digit is the same)
9) $0.1001 < 0.101$ (since $0.100 < 0.101$)
10) $0.04000 = 0.04$ (Sec. 2.1)
11) $6.012 > 6$ (since $6 = 6.000$ and $6.012 > 6.000$)
12) $0.0303 > 0.03003$ (since $0.0303 > 0.0300$)

Exercise Set 2.5

1) $0.5 > 0.05$ (tenths > hundredths)
2) $0.35 < 0.57$ (since $0.3 < 0.5$)
3) $0.009 > 0.0009$ (thousandths > ten thousandths)
4) $2.65 > 2.6$ (since $2.6 = 2.60$ and $2.65 > 2.60$)
5) $0.0456 < 0.053$ (since $0.04 < 0.05$)
6) $0.02 < 0.1$ (since hundredths < tenths)
7) $1.1 > 0.7$ (since units > tenths)
8) $0.269 > 0.268$
9) $0.0434 < 0.434$ (since hundredths < tenths)
10) $0.01 = 0.010$ (Sec. 2.1)
11) $0.22 > 0.202$ (since $0.22 = 0.220$ and $0.220 > 0.202$)
12) $0.47 < 0.5$ (since $0.4 < 0.5$)
13) $8.546 < 8.564$ (since $8.54 < 8.56$)
14) $0.0971 < 0.09712$ (since $0.0971 = 0.09710$ and $0.09710 < 0.09712$)
15) $0.67337 < 0.6734$ (since $0.6733 < 0.6734$)
16) $8.25149 < 8.2515$ (since $8.2514 < 8.2515$)
17) $0.000067 < 0.00021$ (since hundred thousandths < ten thousandths)
18) $9.0999 < 9.1$ (since $9.0 < 9.1$)

Exercise Set 2.6

1) $0.4 < 0.5 < 0.6$
2) $0.003 < 0.02 < 0.1$ (thousandths < hundredths < tenths)
3) $0.59 < 0.6 < 0.61$ (since $0.59 < 0.60 < 0.61$)
4) $0.07 < 0.075 < 0.08$ (since $0.070 < 0.075 < 0.080$)
5) $0.44 < 0.442 < 0.444$ (since $0.440 < 0.442$)
6) $2.34 < 2.35 < 2.43$
7) $0.707 < 0.7071 < 0.71$ (since $0.7070 < 0.7071 < 0.7100$)
8) $0.000289 < 0.000290 < 0.0017$ (these were already in order)
Notes: $0.000289 < 0.000290$ and ten thousandths < thousandths
9) $49.9 < 50 < 50.5$ (since $49.9 < 50.0 < 50.5$)
10) $0.09 < 0.091 < 0.1$ (since $0.090 < 0.091$ and hundredths < tenths)

Exercise Set 2.7

1) $0.05 < 0.06 < 0.065 < 0.5$ (since $0.050 < 0.060 < 0.065 < 0.500$)
2) $1.1 < 1.11 < 1.2 < 1.212$ (since $1.100 < 1.110 < 1.200 < 1.212$)
3) $0.007 < 0.009 < 0.03 < 0.1$ (since thousandths < hundredths < tenths)
4) $0.006 < 0.01 < 0.025 < 0.2$ (since thousandths < hundredths < tenths)
5) $4.097 < 4.238 < 4.24 < 4.242$ (since $4.24 = 4.240$)
6) $0.001 < 0.0015 < 0.01 < 0.015$ (since $0.0010 < 0.0015 < 0.0100 < 0.0150$)
7) $0.4632 < 0.6324 < 0.6342 < 0.6432$
8) $1.00062 < 1.0054 < 1.048 < 1.1$ (these were already in order)
9) $0.0078 < 0.0087 < 0.07 < 0.08$ (since thousandths < hundredths)
10) $0.49 < 0.499 < 0.5 < 0.501$ (since $0.490 < 0.499 < 0.500 < 0.501$)
11) $1.999 < 2 < 2.09 < 2.1$ (since $1.999 < 2.000 < 2.090 < 2.100$)
12) $6.54201 < 6.54211 < 6.54223 < 6.543$ (since $6.543 = 6.54300$)

Chapter 3 Add and Subtract Decimals

Exercise Set 3.1

1)
$$\begin{array}{r} 0.4 \\ + 0.2 \\ \hline 0.6 \end{array}$$

2)
$$\begin{array}{r} 0.7 \\ + 0.6 \\ \hline 1.3 \end{array}$$

3)
$$\begin{array}{r} 0.09 \\ + 0.10 \\ \hline 0.19 \end{array}$$

4)
$$\begin{array}{r} 0.08 \\ + 0.07 \\ \hline 0.15 \end{array}$$

5)
$$\begin{array}{r} 0.30 \\ + 0.06 \\ \hline 0.36 \end{array}$$

6)
$$\begin{array}{r} 0.008 \\ + 0.005 \\ \hline 0.013 \end{array}$$

7)
$$\begin{array}{r} 0.6 \\ + 0.4 \\ \hline 1.0 \end{array}$$

8)
$$\begin{array}{r} 0.09 \\ + 0.09 \\ \hline 0.18 \end{array}$$

9)
$$\begin{array}{r} 2.0 \\ + 0.8 \\ \hline 2.8 \end{array}$$

10)
$$\begin{array}{r} 0.40 \\ + 0.04 \\ \hline 0.44 \end{array}$$

11)
$$\begin{array}{r} 0.07 \\ + 0.05 \\ \hline 0.12 \end{array}$$

12)
$$\begin{array}{r} 0.009 \\ + 0.060 \\ \hline 0.069 \end{array}$$

Note: The answer to Problem 7 is simply 1 (recall from Sec. 2.1 that a trailing decimal zero does not affect the value of a number such that 1 and 1.0 are equivalent).

13)
$$\begin{array}{r} 0.8 \\ + 0.6 \\ \hline 1.4 \end{array}$$

14)
$$\begin{array}{r} 0.70 \\ + 0.04 \\ \hline 0.74 \end{array}$$

15)
$$\begin{array}{r} 0.05 \\ + 0.05 \\ \hline 0.10 \end{array}$$

16)
$$\begin{array}{r} 0.06 \\ + 0.20 \\ \hline 0.26 \end{array}$$

17)
$$\begin{array}{r} 0.09 \\ + 0.08 \\ \hline 0.17 \end{array}$$

18)
$$\begin{array}{r} 1.0 \\ + 0.4 \\ \hline 1.4 \end{array}$$

Note: The answer to Problem 15 is simply 0.1 (recall from Sec. 2.1 that a trailing decimal zero does not affect the value of a number such that 0.1 and 0.10 are equivalent).

Master Decimals Math Practice Workbook with Answers

Exercise Set 3.2

1)
$$0.9 - 0.3 = 0.6$$

2)
$$1.2 - 0.5 = 0.7$$

3)
$$0.10 - 0.04 = 0.06$$

4)
$$0.08 - 0.06 = 0.02$$

5)
$$0.15 - 0.07 = 0.08$$

6)
$$0.20 - 0.09 = 0.11$$

7)
$$0.83 - 0.20 = 0.63$$

8)
$$0.007 - 0.003 = 0.004$$

9)
$$1.4 - 0.7 = 0.7$$

10)
$$1.0 - 0.5 = 0.5$$

11)
$$0.012 - 0.004 = 0.008$$

12)
$$0.10 - 0.01 = 0.09$$

13)
$$0.8 - 0.4 = 0.4$$

14)
$$0.63 - 0.30 = 0.33$$

15)
$$1.1 - 0.5 = 0.6$$

16)
$$0.60 - 0.04 = 0.56$$

17)
$$1.7 - 0.7 = 1.0$$

18)
$$0.040 - 0.003 = 0.037$$

Note: The answer to Problem 17 is simply 1 (Sec. 2.1).

Exercise Set 3.3

1) $0.8 + 0.7 = 1.5$

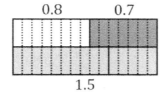

Answer Key

2) $2.4 + 1.6 = 4$

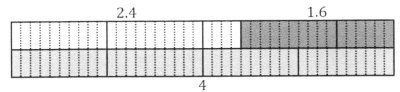

3) $1.9 + 1.4 = 3.3$

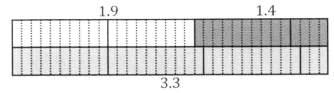

Exercise Set 3.4

1) $2 - 1.3 = 0.7$

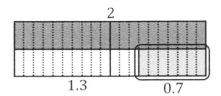

2) $2.5 - 0.7 = 1.8$

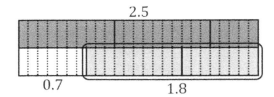

Exercise Set 3.5

1)
$$\begin{array}{r} 4.5 \\ +\,2.3 \\ \hline 6.8 \end{array}$$

2)
$$\begin{array}{r} \overset{1}{}0.70 \\ +\,0.58 \\ \hline 1.28 \end{array}$$

3)
$$\begin{array}{r} \overset{1}{}\overset{1}{0}.851 \\ +\,0.463 \\ \hline 1.314 \end{array}$$

4)
$$\begin{array}{r} 2.60 \\ +\,0.35 \\ \hline 2.95 \end{array}$$

Master Decimals Math Practice Workbook with Answers

5)
$$\begin{array}{r} \overset{1}{}2.74 \\ +\,0.90 \\ \hline 3.64 \end{array}$$

6)
$$\begin{array}{r} \overset{1\,1}{0.579} \\ +\,0.041 \\ \hline 0.620 \end{array}$$

7)
$$\begin{array}{r} 0.61 \\ +\,0.30 \\ \hline 0.91 \end{array}$$

8)
$$\begin{array}{r} 6.0 \\ +\,1.5 \\ \hline 7.5 \end{array}$$

9)
$$\begin{array}{r} \overset{1}{}2.4 \\ +\,0.6 \\ \hline 3.0 \end{array}$$

10)
$$\begin{array}{r} \overset{1}{0.089} \\ +\,0.050 \\ \hline 0.139 \end{array}$$

11)
$$\begin{array}{r} \overset{1\,1}{39.7} \\ +\,18.4 \\ \hline 58.1 \end{array}$$

12)
$$\begin{array}{r} \overset{1\,1}{9.900} \\ +\,0.101 \\ \hline 10.001 \end{array}$$

Note: The answers to Problems 6 and 9 are 0.62 and 3 (recall Sec. 2.1).

13)
$$\begin{array}{r} \overset{1}{0.56} \\ +\,0.39 \\ \hline 0.95 \end{array}$$

14)
$$\begin{array}{r} 0.63 \\ +\,0.30 \\ \hline 0.93 \end{array}$$

15)
$$\begin{array}{r} \overset{1}{5.82} \\ +\,0.25 \\ \hline 6.07 \end{array}$$

16)
$$\begin{array}{r} \overset{1}{6.80} \\ +\,0.73 \\ \hline 7.53 \end{array}$$

17)
$$\begin{array}{r} \overset{1}{0.080} \\ +\,0.057 \\ \hline 0.137 \end{array}$$

18)
$$\begin{array}{r} \overset{1\,1}{28.7} \\ +\,8.4 \\ \hline 37.1 \end{array}$$

19)
$$\begin{array}{r} \overset{1}{0.470} \\ +\,0.082 \\ \hline 0.552 \end{array}$$

20)
$$\begin{array}{r} \overset{1}{73.5} \\ +\,0.5 \\ \hline 74.0 \end{array}$$

21)
$$\begin{array}{r} 0.4040 \\ +\,0.0202 \\ \hline 0.4242 \end{array}$$

22)
$$\begin{array}{r} \overset{1\,1}{7.36} \\ +\,5.81 \\ \hline 13.17 \end{array}$$

23)
$$\begin{array}{r} \overset{1}{1.490} \\ +\,0.378 \\ \hline 1.868 \end{array}$$

24)
$$\begin{array}{r} \overset{1\,1}{0.078} \\ +\,0.032 \\ \hline 0.110 \end{array}$$

25)
$$\begin{array}{r} \overset{1\,1}{99.880} \\ +\,1.111 \\ \hline 100.991 \end{array}$$

26)
$$\begin{array}{r} \overset{1\,1}{0.634} \\ +\,0.189 \\ \hline 0.823 \end{array}$$

27)
$$\begin{array}{r} \overset{1}{14.99} \\ +\,0.20 \\ \hline 15.19 \end{array}$$

Answer Key

Note: The answers to Problems 20 and 24 are 74 and 0.11 (recall Sec. 2.1).

Exercise Set 3.6

1)
$$\begin{array}{r} {}^{6\ 12}\\ 0.7\cancel{2}\\ -\ 0.24\\ \hline 0.48 \end{array}$$

2)
$$\begin{array}{r} {}^{7\ 14}\\ 8.\cancel{4}6\\ -\ 0.90\\ \hline 7.56 \end{array}$$

3)
$$\begin{array}{r} {}^{5\ 10}\\ 0.0\cancel{6}\cancel{0}\\ -\ 0.015\\ \hline 0.045 \end{array}$$

4)
$$\begin{array}{r} {}^{6\ 11}\\ 0.7\cancel{1}6\\ -\ 0.542\\ \hline 0.174 \end{array}$$

5)
$$\begin{array}{r} {}^{6\ 13}\\ 0.0\cancel{7}\cancel{3}\\ -\ 0.046\\ \hline 0.027 \end{array}$$

6)
$$\begin{array}{r} {}^{5\ 11}\\ 0.3\cancel{6}\cancel{1}\\ -\ 0.222\\ \hline 0.139 \end{array}$$

7)
$$\begin{array}{r} {}^{5\ 13\ 13}\\ 6.\cancel{4}\cancel{3}\\ -\ 3.59\\ \hline 2.84 \end{array}$$

8)
$$\begin{array}{r} 0.0096\\ -\ 0.0060\\ \hline 0.0036 \end{array}$$

9)
$$\begin{array}{r} {}^{5\ 13}\\ 6\cancel{3}.5\\ -\ 27.2\\ \hline 36.3 \end{array}$$

10)
$$\begin{array}{r} {}^{3\ 12}\\ 4.\cancel{2}36\\ -\ 1.536\\ \hline 2.700 \end{array}$$

11)
$$\begin{array}{r} {}^{0\ 12}\\ 1.\cancel{2}56\\ -\ 0.843\\ \hline 0.413 \end{array}$$

12)
$$\begin{array}{r} {}^{7\ 9\ 9\ 10}\\ 8.\cancel{0}\cancel{0}\cancel{0}\\ -\ 0.125\\ \hline 7.875 \end{array}$$

Note: The answer to Problem 10 is simply 2.7 since 2.7 and 2.700 are equivalent (Sec. 2.1).

13)
$$\begin{array}{r} {}^{4\ 16}\\ 5.\cancel{6}\\ -\ 4.9\\ \hline 0.7 \end{array}$$

14)
$$\begin{array}{r} {}^{6\ 10}\\ 0.7\cancel{0}\\ -\ 0.23\\ \hline 0.47 \end{array}$$

15)
$$\begin{array}{r} 1.41\\ -\ 0.41\\ \hline 1.00 \end{array}$$

16)
$$\begin{array}{r} {}^{6\ 13}\\ 0.\cancel{7}\cancel{3}6\\ -\ 0.285\\ \hline 0.451 \end{array}$$

17)
$$\begin{array}{r} {}^{0\ 13}\\ 1\cancel{3}.8\\ -\ 5.3\\ \hline 8.5 \end{array}$$

18)
$$\begin{array}{r} 0.097\\ -\ 0.080\\ \hline 0.017 \end{array}$$

19)
$$\begin{array}{r} {}^{5\ 10}\\ 0.6\cancel{0}\\ -\ 0.25\\ \hline 0.35 \end{array}$$

20)
$$\begin{array}{r} {}^{7\ 14}\\ 8.\cancel{4}5\\ -\ 3.70\\ \hline 4.75 \end{array}$$

21)
$$\begin{array}{r} {}^{4\ 17\ 11}\\ 0.\cancel{5}\cancel{8}\cancel{1}\\ -\ 0.492\\ \hline 0.089 \end{array}$$

Note: The answer to Problem 15 is simply the whole number 1, since 1 and 1.00 are equivalent (Sec. 2.1).

22)
```
  1 9 10
  2.00
- 0.79
  ─────
  1.21
```

23)
```
    8 12
  0.9̸2̸6
- 0.543
  ─────
  0.383
```

24)
```
     7 10
  0.038̸0̸
- 0.0067
  ──────
  0.0313
```

25)
```
  0.449
- 0.320
  ─────
  0.129
```

26)
```
  0 10 10
  0.1̸1̸0̸
- 0.027
  ─────
  0.083
```

27)
```
  0 17 15 13
  1.8̸6̸3̸
- 0.985
  ─────
  0.878
```

Exercise Set 3.7

1) $10.25 - 2.75 = 7.50 = 7.5$ feet

Note: You should stack the numbers vertically like we have done throughout the chapter.

2) $2.8 + 1.5 = 4.3$ miles

3) $9.03 - 0.26 = 8.77$ seconds

4) $\$1.75 + \$1.50 + \$0.85 = \$3.25 + \$0.85 = \$4.10$ (four dollars and ten cents)

Note: With money, we usually keep a trailing zero in the hundredths place, which is why we wrote $4.10 instead of $4.1.

5) $5 - 1.6 - 2.7 = 3.4 - 2.7 = 0.7$ feet

Alternate solution: $1.6 + 2.7 = 4.3$ and $5 - 4.3 = 0.7$ feet

6) $17.2 - 4.9 = 12.3$ ounces

7) $\$1.85 + \$1.55 = \$3.40$ (see the note in the solution to Problem 4)

Note: This word problem is unusual in that the question asked for the "difference" yet the solution required "addition." If the problem had given the prices of a large popcorn and a small popcorn, then we would have subtracted to find the difference. Instead, this problem gave us two differences and we added these differences together to find the combined difference.

Chapter 4 Multiply Decimals

Exercise Set 4.1

1) $0.2 \times 10 = 2$ (shift the decimal point 1 place to the right)
2) $0.7 \times 0.1 = 0.07$ (shift the decimal point 1 place to the left)
3) $6.4 \times 100 = 640$ (shift the decimal point 2 places to the right)
4) $1.8 \times 0.01 = 0.018$ (shift the decimal point 2 places to the left)
5) $0.035 \times 1000 = 35$ (shift the decimal point 3 places to the right)
6) $0.099 \times 0.001 = 0.000099$ (shift the decimal point 3 places to the left)
7) $27.3 \times 100 = 2730$ (shift the decimal point 2 places to the right)
8) $0.496 \times 0.1 = 0.0496$ (shift the decimal point 1 place to the left)
9) $0.008 \times 10 = 0.08$ (shift the decimal point 1 place to the right)
10) $937 \times 0.01 = 9.37$ (shift the decimal point 2 places to the left)
11) $0.016 \times 10{,}000 = 160$ (shift the decimal point 4 places to the right)
12) $5.963 \times 100 = 596.3$ (shift the decimal point 2 places to the right)
13) $0.01 \times 0.001 = 0.00001$ (shift the decimal point 3 places to the left)
14) $25 \times 0.0001 = 0.0025$ (shift the decimal point 4 places to the left)
15) $0.967 \times 100{,}000 = 96{,}700$ (shift the decimal point 5 places to the right)
16) $0.0023 \times 1000 = 2.3$ (shift the decimal point 3 places to the right)
17) $0.42 \times 0.01 = 0.0042$ (shift the decimal point 2 places to the left)
18) $63.84 \times 0.001 = 0.06384$ (shift the decimal point 3 places to the left)
19) $0.0003 \times 1{,}000{,}000 = 300$ (shift the decimal point 6 places to the right)
20) $0.846 \times 0.00001 = 0.00000846$ (shift the decimal point 5 places to the left)

Exercise Set 4.2

1)
```
    1
   7.3
  × 6
  ────
  43.8
```

2)
```
      2
   0.65
  ×  4
  ────
   2.60
```

3)
```
     2
   24.1
  ×  7
  ────
  168.7
```

4)
```
    2 2
   5.87
  ×  3
  ────
  17.61
```

Note: The answer to Problem 2 is 2.6 (Sec. 2.1).

5)	6)	7)	8)
1 1	2 4	1 1	5
0.444	53.6	9.85	0.086
× 3	× 8	× 2	× 9
1.332	428.8	19.70	0.774

9)	10)	11)	12)
3 2	4	3	1 3 3
87.4	0.906	21.6	34.79
× 5	× 7	× 6	× 4
437.0	6.342	129.6	139.16

Note: The answers to Problems 7 and 9 are 19.7 and 437 (Sec. 2.1).

13)	14)	15)	16)
1 1	3 2	2	4 3
7.65	84.3	9.27	0.454
× 2	× 8	× 3	× 9
15.30	674.4	27.81	4.086

17)	18)	19)	20)
3 1 5	3 2	2 4	4 2 6
0.7416	5.604	24.08	9.629
× 9	× 6	× 5	× 7
6.6744	33.624	120.40	67.403

21)	22)	23)	24)
4 2 5	6 5 2	2 1	7 7
56.38	486.3	5.641	0.9078
× 7	× 8	× 4	× 9
394.66	3890.4	22.564	8.1702

Note: The answers to Problems 13 and 19 are 15.3 and 120.4 (Sec. 2.1).

Exercise Set 4.3

1)	2)	3)	4)	
1	4	6	2	Note that the second
2	2		1	number is a whole
3.6	0.49	1.8	0.63	number; it does **not**
× 2 4	× 5 3	× 8 1	× 7 4	have a decimal
14.4	1.47	1.8	2.52	point.
72.0	24.50	144.0	44.10	
86.4	25.97	145.8	46.62	

Answer Key

5)
```
   2
   4
  0.57
× 36
─────
  3.42
 17.10
─────
 20.52
```

6)
```
    2
  1.04
× 16
─────
  6.24
 10.40
─────
 16.64
```

7)
```
   2
   4
   7.5
×  49
─────
  67.5
 300.0
─────
 367.5
```

8)
```
   1 1
  22.2
×  90
─────
   0.0
1998.0
──────
1998.0
```

Note that the second number is a whole number; it does **not** have a decimal point.

Note: The answer to Problem 8 is 1998 (Sec. 2.1).

9)
```
  2 1
  94.3
×  62
──────
 188.6
5658.0
──────
5846.6
```

10)
```
  0.081
×   78
──────
  0.648
  5.670
──────
  6.318
```

11)
```
   2 3
   2 3
   45.6
×   55
──────
  228.0
 2280.0
──────
 2508.0
```

12)
```
   1 1
   4 5
   3.68
×   27
──────
  25.76
  73.60
──────
  99.36
```

13)
```
  6.2
× 11
─────
  6.2
 62.0
─────
 68.2
```

14)
```
    7
  0.29
× 80
─────
  0.00
 23.20
─────
 23.20
```

15)
```
    4
    2
  0.018
×   63
──────
  0.054
  1.080
──────
  1.134
```

16)
```
    1
    1
   7.4
×  34
─────
  29.6
 222.0
─────
 251.6
```

Note: The answers to Problems 11 and 14 are 2508 and 23.2 (Sec. 2.1).

17)
```
   2
   4
  0.57
× 46
─────
  3.42
 22.80
─────
 26.22
```

18)
```
   6 2
   4 1
   3.73
×  96
──────
  22.38
 335.70
──────
 358.08
```

19)
```
    1
    4
   9.5
×  29
─────
  85.5
 190.0
─────
 275.5
```

20)
```
   6 4
   4 3
  88.6
×  75
──────
 443.0
6202.0
──────
6645.0
```

Note that the second number is a whole number; it does **not** have a decimal point.

21)
```
    4
    1
   4.91
×  52
──────
   9.82
 245.50
──────
 255.32
```

22)
```
     4
     4
  0.0077
×   77
──────
  0.0539
  0.5390
──────
  0.5929
```

23)
```
   4 7
   2 4
  0.659
×  85
──────
  3.295
 52.720
──────
 56.015
```

24)
```
   8 1
   7 1
   9.92
×  98
──────
  79.36
 892.80
──────
 972.16
```

Note: The answer to Problem 20 is 6645 (Sec. 2.1).

Master Decimals Math Practice Workbook with Answers

Exercise Set 4.4

1) $0.6 \times 0.3 = 0.18$ (2 decimal places)
2) $0.2 \times 0.08 = 0.016$ (3 decimal places)
3) $0.004 \times 0.7 = 0.0028$ (4 decimal places)
4) $0.03 \times 0.2 = 0.006$ (3 decimal places)
5) $0.04 \times 0.006 = 0.00024$ (5 decimal places)
6) $0.8 \times 0.05 = 0.040 = 0.04$ (3 decimal places before removing the trailing zero)
7) $0.5 \times 0.5 = 0.25$ (2 decimal places)
8) $0.003 \times 0.3 = 0.0009$ (4 decimal places)
9) $0.09 \times 0.4 = 0.036$ (3 decimal places)
10) $0.08 \times 0.07 = 0.0056$ (4 decimal places)
11) $0.2 \times 0.00002 = 0.000004$ (6 decimal places)
12) $0.9 \times 0.09 = 0.081$ (3 decimal places)
13) $0.4 \times 0.005 = 0.0020 = 0.002$ (4 decimal places before removing the trailing zero)
14) $0.0002 \times 0.06 = 0.000012$ (6 decimal places)
15) $0.07 \times 0.07 = 0.0049$ (4 decimal places)
16) $0.4 \times 0.3 = 0.12$ (2 decimal places)
17) $0.004 \times 0.0002 = 0.0000008$ (7 decimal places)
18) $0.006 \times 0.09 = 0.00054$ (5 decimal places)
19) $0.05 \times 0.6 = 0.030 = 0.03$ (3 decimal places before removing the trailing zero)
20) $0.0007 \times 0.0001 = 0.00000007$ (8 decimal places)
21) $0.00009 \times 0.7 = 0.000063$ (6 decimal places)
22) $0.2 \times 0.06 = 0.012$ (3 decimal places)
23) $0.008 \times 0.08 = 0.00064$ (5 decimal places)
24) $0.03 \times 0.04 = 0.0012$ (4 decimal places)
25) $0.7 \times 0.006 = 0.0042$ (4 decimal places)
26) $0.009 \times 0.008 = 0.000072$ (6 decimal places)

Answer Key

Exercise Set 4.5

1) $0.2 \times 0.8 = 0.16$

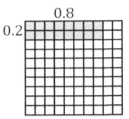

2) $0.6 \times 0.6 = 0.36$

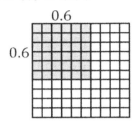

3) $0.9 \times 0.4 = 0.36$

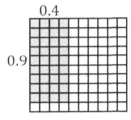

4) $0.3 \times 0.7 = 0.21$

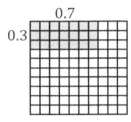

5) $0.8 \times 0.6 = 0.48$

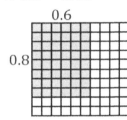

6) $0.7 \times 0.9 = 0.63$

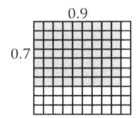

Exercise Set 4.6

1)
$$\begin{array}{r} {\scriptstyle 2} \\ 0.78 \\ \times\, 0.3 \\ \hline 0.234 \end{array}$$

2)
$$\begin{array}{r} {\scriptstyle 2} \\ 9.4 \\ \times\, 0.06 \\ \hline 0.564 \end{array}$$

3)
$$\begin{array}{r} {\scriptstyle 2\ 2} \\ 0.465 \\ \times\, 0.4 \\ \hline 0.1860 \end{array}$$

4)
$$\begin{array}{r} {\scriptstyle 1\ 4} \\ 2.17 \\ \times\, 0.007 \\ \hline 0.01519 \end{array}$$

5)
$$\begin{array}{r} {\scriptstyle 2\ 4} \\ 52.6 \\ \times\, 0.08 \\ \hline 4.208 \end{array}$$

6)
$$\begin{array}{r} {\scriptstyle 1} \\ 0.383 \\ \times\, 0.2 \\ \hline 0.0766 \end{array}$$

7)
$$\begin{array}{r} {\scriptstyle 4\ 3} \\ 1.97 \\ \times\, 0.005 \\ \hline 0.00985 \end{array}$$

8)
$$\begin{array}{r} {\scriptstyle 4\ 7} \\ 0.0648 \\ \times\, 0.9 \\ \hline 0.05832 \end{array}$$

Note: The answer to Problem 3 is 0.186 (Sec. 2.1).

9)
$$\begin{array}{r} 8.02 \\ \times\, 0.1 \\ \hline 0.802 \end{array}$$

10)
$$\begin{array}{r} {\scriptstyle 1\ 1} \\ 22.2 \\ \times\, 0.0007 \\ \hline 0.01554 \end{array}$$

11)
$$\begin{array}{r} {\scriptstyle 1\ 3} \\ 0.925 \\ \times\, 0.06 \\ \hline 0.05550 \end{array}$$

12)
$$\begin{array}{r} {\scriptstyle 1\ 2} \\ 404.7 \\ \times\, 0.3 \\ \hline 121.41 \end{array}$$

13)
$$\begin{array}{r} {\scriptstyle 1\ 1\ 3} \\ 142.9 \\ \times\, 0.04 \\ \hline 5.716 \end{array}$$

14)
$$\begin{array}{r} {\scriptstyle 2\ \ \ 7} \\ 6.308 \\ \times\, 0.9 \\ \hline 5.6772 \end{array}$$

15)
$$\begin{array}{r} {\scriptstyle 7\ 1\ 4} \\ 0.5915 \\ \times\, 0.008 \\ \hline 0.0047320 \end{array}$$

16)
$$\begin{array}{r} {\scriptstyle 3\ 3\ 1} \\ 37.72 \\ \times\, 0.05 \\ \hline 1.8860 \end{array}$$

Note: The answers to Problems 11, 15, and 16 are 0.0555, 0.004732, and 1.886 (Sec. 2.1).

17)
$$\begin{array}{r} {\scriptstyle 3\ 5\ 1} \\ 0.4593 \\ \times\, 0.06 \\ \hline 0.027558 \end{array}$$

18)
$$\begin{array}{r} {\scriptstyle 1\ 1} \\ 0.08296 \\ \times\, 0.002 \\ \hline 0.00016592 \end{array}$$

19)
$$\begin{array}{r} {\scriptstyle 2} \\ 20.71 \\ \times\, 0.3 \\ \hline 6.213 \end{array}$$

20)
$$\begin{array}{r} 7.804 \\ \times\, 0.001 \\ \hline 0.007804 \end{array}$$

21)
$$\begin{array}{r} {\scriptstyle 3\ 1} \\ 0.003162 \\ \times\, 0.5 \\ \hline 0.0015810 \end{array}$$

22)
$$\begin{array}{r} {\scriptstyle 4\ 4\ 4} \\ 55.55 \\ \times\, 0.08 \\ \hline 4.4440 \end{array}$$

23)
$$\begin{array}{r} {\scriptstyle 3\ 2\ 6} \\ 6.439 \\ \times\, 0.007 \\ \hline 0.045073 \end{array}$$

24)
$$\begin{array}{r} {\scriptstyle 5\ 3\ 6} \\ 963.7 \\ \times\, 0.9 \\ \hline 867.33 \end{array}$$

Note: The answers to Problems 21-22 are 0.001581 and 4.444 (Sec. 2.1).

Exercise Set 4.7

1)
$$\begin{array}{r} {\scriptstyle 2} \\ {\scriptstyle 1} \\ 7.4 \\ \times\, 5.3 \\ \hline 2.2\,2 \\ 3\,7.0\,0 \\ \hline 3\,9.2\,2 \end{array}$$

2)
$$\begin{array}{r} {\scriptstyle 1} \\ 0.8\,3 \\ \times\, 0.2\,6 \\ \hline 0.0\,4\,9\,8 \\ 0.1\,6\,6\,0 \\ \hline 0.2\,1\,5\,8 \end{array}$$

3)
$$\begin{array}{r} {\scriptstyle 6} \\ {\scriptstyle 3} \\ 0.5\,9 \\ \times\, 7.4 \\ \hline 0.2\,3\,6 \\ 4.1\,3\,0 \\ \hline 4.3\,6\,6 \end{array}$$

4)
$$\begin{array}{r} 3.6 \\ \times\, 0.0\,1\,1 \\ \hline 0.0\,0\,3\,6 \\ 0.0\,3\,6\,0 \\ \hline 0.0\,3\,9\,6 \end{array}$$

Answer Key

5)
```
      4.1
   × 0.6 2
   ─────────
    0.0 8 2
    2.4 6 0
   ─────────
    2.5 4 2
```

6)
```
       ¹
       ⁴
    0.0 2 5
    × 3.8
   ─────────
    0.0 2 0 0
    0.0 7 5 0
   ─────────
    0.0 9 5 0
```

7)
```
       ⁷
       ³
     0.1 8
   × 0.0 9 4
   ─────────
    0.0 0 0 7 2
    0.0 1 6 2 0
   ─────────
    0.0 1 6 9 2
```

8)
```
      ⁵ ⁵
      ³ ³
      9 6.7
    × 8.5
   ─────────
    4 8.3 5
    7 7 3.6 0
   ─────────
    8 2 1.9 5
```

9)
```
       ²
       ²
      6.5 2
   × 0.0 0 4 4
   ─────────
    0.0 0 2 6 0 8
    0.0 2 6 0 8 0
   ─────────
    0.0 2 8 6 8 8
```

10)
```
         ⁷
      0.3 0 8
    × 0.0 1 9
   ─────────
    0.0 0 2 7 7 2
    0.0 0 3 0 8 0
   ─────────
    0.0 0 5 8 5 2
```

11)
```
      ³ ³
      ⁴ ⁴
      7.6 7
    × 0.5 7
   ─────────
    0.5 3 6 9
    3.8 3 5 0
   ─────────
    4.3 7 1 9
```

12)
```
      ¹ ¹
      ⁴ ⁴
      3.6 8
    × 2.6
   ─────────
    2.2 0 8
    7.3 6 0
   ─────────
    9.5 6 8
```

Note: The answer to Problem 6 is 0.095 (Sec. 2.1).

13)
```
       ³
       ²
     0.0 5 5
    × 7.5
   ─────────
    0.0 2 7 5
    0.3 8 5 0
   ─────────
    0.4 1 2 5
```

14)
```
       ²
      9.3
    × 0.9 3
   ─────────
    0.2 7 9
    8.3 7 0
   ─────────
    8.6 4 9
```

15)
```
       ¹
       ³
     0.0 0 4 4
    × 4.8
   ─────────
    0.0 0 3 5 2
    0.0 1 7 6 0
   ─────────
    0.0 2 1 1 2
```

16)
```
       ³
      0.2 6
    × 0.6 1
   ─────────
    0.0 0 2 6
    0.1 5 6 0
   ─────────
    0.1 5 8 6
```

17)
```
       ²
       ⁶
     0.0 0 1 9
    × 0.3 7
   ─────────
    0.0 0 0 1 3 3
    0.0 0 0 5 7 0
   ─────────
    0.0 0 0 7 0 3
```

18)
```
      8.1
    × 6.2
   ─────────
     1.6 2
    4 8.6 0
   ─────────
    5 0.2 2
```

19)
```
      ⁷ ⁶
      ² ²
     0.0 6 8 8
    × 0.0 8 3
   ─────────
    0.0 0 0 2 0 6 4
    0.0 0 5 5 0 4 0
   ─────────
    0.0 0 5 7 1 0 4
```

20)
```
      ² ⁶
      ² ⁶
      4.2 7
    × 0.0 0 9 9
   ─────────
    0.0 0 3 8 4 3
    0.0 3 8 4 3 0
   ─────────
    0.0 4 2 2 7 3
```

21)
```
       ⁷ ¹
      0.3 9 2
    × 0.0 0 1 8
   ─────────
    0.0 0 0 3 1 3 6
    0.0 0 0 3 9 2 0
   ─────────
    0.0 0 0 7 0 5 6
```

22)
```
      ² ³
      ¹ ²
      0.7 4 6
    × 0.0 5 4
   ─────────
    0.0 0 2 9 8 4
    0.0 3 7 3 0 0
   ─────────
    0.0 4 0 2 8 4
```

23)
```
      ¹ ¹
      ⁵ ³
      9.8 5
    × 2.6
   ─────────
    5.9 1 0
    1 9.7 0 0
   ─────────
    2 5.6 1 0
```

24)
```
      ¹ ¹
      ² ²
     0.0 0 8 3 4
    × 0.0 4 7
   ─────────
    0.0 0 0 0 5 8 3 8
    0.0 0 0 3 3 3 6 0
   ─────────
    0.0 0 0 3 9 1 9 8
```

Note: The answer to Problem 23 is 25.61 (Sec. 2.1).

Exercise Set 4.8

1) $0.8 \times 7.6 = 0.8 \times (7 + 0.6) = 0.8 \times 7 + 0.8 \times 0.6 = 5.6 + 0.48 = \boxed{6.08}$
2) $5 \times 4.9 = 5 \times (4 + 0.9) = 5 \times 4 + 5 \times 0.9 = 20 + 4.5 = \boxed{24.5}$
3) $0.6 \times 0.37 = 0.6 \times (0.3 + 0.07) = 0.6 \times 0.3 + 0.6 \times 0.07$
$= 0.18 + 0.042 = \boxed{0.222}$
4) $0.04 \times 5.2 = 0.04 \times (5 + 0.2) = 0.04 \times 5 + 0.04 \times 0.2$
$= 0.20 + 0.008 = \boxed{0.208}$
5) $0.002 \times 0.61 = 0.002 \times (0.6 + 0.01) = 0.002 \times 0.6 + 0.002 \times 0.01$
$= 0.0012 + 0.00002 = \boxed{0.00122}$
6) $9.7 \times 8 = (9 + 0.7) \times 8 = 9 \times 8 + 0.7 \times 8 = 72 + 5.6 = \boxed{77.6}$
7) $0.48 \times 0.5 = (0.4 + 0.08) \times 0.5 = 0.4 \times 0.5 + 0.08 \times 0.5 = 0.20 + 0.040 = \boxed{0.24}$
8) $0.072 \times 0.03 = (0.07 + 0.002) \times 0.03 = 0.07 \times 0.03 + 0.002 \times 0.03$
$= 0.0021 + 0.00006 = \boxed{0.00216}$
9) $4 \times 6.57 = 4 \times (6 + 0.5 + 0.07) = 4 \times 6 + 4 \times 0.5 + 4 \times 0.07$
$= 24 + 2 + 0.28 = \boxed{26.28}$
Note: For most of these problems, it would be wise to add the numbers like we did in Chapter 3 (by stacking the numbers vertically, aligned at their decimal points).
10) $0.9 \times 0.192 = 0.9 \times (0.1 + 0.09 + 0.002)$
$= 0.9 \times 0.1 + 0.9 \times 0.09 + 0.9 \times 0.002 = 0.09 + 0.081 + 0.0018 = \boxed{0.1728}$
11) $0.08 \times 7.33 = 0.08 \times (7 + 0.3 + 0.03) = 0.08 \times 7 + 0.08 \times 0.3 + 0.08 \times 0.03$
$= 0.56 + 0.024 + 0.0024 = \boxed{0.5864}$
12) $63.4 \times 0.5 = (60 + 3 + 0.4) \times 0.5 = 60 \times 0.5 + 3 \times 0.5 + 0.4 \times 0.5$
$= 30 + 1.5 + 0.20 = \boxed{31.7}$

Exercise Set 4.9

1) $1.8 \times 1.4 = 1 \times 1 + 0.8 \times 1 + 1 \times 0.4 + 0.8 \times 0.4 = 1 + 0.8 + 0.4 + 0.32 = \boxed{2.52}$
Note: For these problems, it would be wise to add the numbers like we did in Chapter 3 (by stacking the numbers vertically, aligned at their decimal points).
2) $4.7 \times 3.6 = 4 \times 3 + 0.7 \times 3 + 4 \times 0.6 + 0.7 \times 0.6 = 12 + 2.1 + 2.4 + 0.42 = \boxed{16.92}$

Answer Key

3) $7.5 \times 8.2 = 7 \times 8 + 0.5 \times 8 + 7 \times 0.2 + 0.5 \times 0.2 = 56 + 4 + 1.4 + 0.1 = \boxed{61.5}$

4) $9.3 \times 0.81 = 9 \times 0.8 + 0.3 \times 0.8 + 9 \times 0.01 + 0.3 \times 0.01$
$= 7.2 + 0.24 + 0.09 + 0.003 = \boxed{7.533}$

5) $0.64 \times 0.29 = 0.6 \times 0.2 + 0.04 \times 0.2 + 0.6 \times 0.09 + 0.04 \times 0.09$
$= 0.12 + 0.008 + 0.054 + 0.0036 = \boxed{0.1856}$

6) $58 \times 0.44 = 50 \times 0.4 + 8 \times 0.4 + 50 \times 0.04 + 8 \times 0.04$
$= 20 + 3.2 + 2 + 0.32 = \boxed{25.52}$

7) $0.037 \times 0.52 = 0.03 \times 0.5 + 0.007 \times 0.5 + 0.03 \times 0.02 + 0.007 \times 0.02$
$= 0.015 + 0.0035 + 0.0006 + 0.00014 = \boxed{0.01924}$

Exercise Set 4.10

1) $3 \times \$5.49 = \$16.47$

Note: You should perform the multiplication like we have in the earlier sections of this chapter, meaning that you should show more work than we have shown here.

2) $12 \times 1.75 = 21.00 = 21$ ounces

3) $5.5 \times 3.75 = 20.625$ square inches

4) $12 \times \$4.95 - \$49.95 = \$59.40 - \$49.95 = \$9.45$

5) $6 \times \$0.54 + 9 \times \$0.68 = \$3.24 + \$6.12 = \$9.36$

6) $d = r \times t = 0.24 \times 3.8 = 0.912$ meters

Note: $r = \frac{d}{t}$ such that $d = r \times t$ (distance equals rate times the elapsed time)

7) $24.5 \times 13.2 = 323.40 = 323.4$ miles

Exercise Set 4.11

1) $0.7^2 = 0.7 \times 0.7 = 0.49$

2) $0.4^3 = 0.4 \times 0.4 \times 0.4 = 0.16 \times 0.4 = 0.064$

3) $0.05^2 = 0.05 \times 0.05 = 0.0025$

4) $0.6^3 = 0.6 \times 0.6 \times 0.6 = 0.36 \times 0.6 = 0.216$

5) $0.8^2 = 0.8 \times 0.8 = 0.64$

6) $0.3^4 = 0.3 \times 0.3 \times 0.3 \times 0.3 = 0.09 \times 0.09 = 0.0081$

7) $0.2^5 = 0.2 \times 0.2 \times 0.2 \times 0.2 \times 0.2 = 0.04 \times 0.04 \times 0.2 = 0.0016 \times 0.2 = 0.00032$

8) $0.01^3 = 0.01 \times 0.01 \times 0.01 = 0.0001 \times 0.01 = 0.000001$

9) $1.4^2 = 1.4 \times 1.4 = 1.96$ (use the method from Sec. 4.7 or 4.9)

10) $0.5^3 = 0.5 \times 0.5 \times 0.5 = 0.25 \times 0.5 = 0.125$

11) $0.04^4 = 0.04 \times 0.04 \times 0.04 \times 0.04 = 0.0016 \times 0.0016 = 0.00000256$

12) $0.06^3 = 0.06 \times 0.06 \times 0.06 = 0.0036 \times 0.06 = 0.000216$

13) $0.27^2 = 0.27 \times 0.27 = 0.0729$ (use the method from Sec. 4.7 or 4.9)

14) $0.1^5 = 0.1 \times 0.1 \times 0.1 \times 0.1 \times 0.1 = 0.01 \times 0.01 \times 0.1 = 0.0001 \times 0.1 = 0.00001$

15) $0.002^3 = 0.002 \times 0.002 \times 0.002 = 0.000004 \times 0.002 = 0.000000008$

16) $0.015^2 = 0.015 \times 0.015 = 0.000225$ (use the method from Sec. 4.7 or 4.9)

17) $0.8^3 = 0.8 \times 0.8 \times 0.8 = 0.64 \times 0.8 = 0.512$

18) $0.07^3 = 0.07 \times 0.07 \times 0.07 = 0.0049 \times 0.07 = 0.000343$

19) $1.4^3 = 1.4 \times 1.4 \times 1.4 = 1.96 \times 1.4 = 2.744$ (use the method from Sec. 4.7 or 4.9)

Exercise Set 4.12

1) $\sqrt{0.25} = \boxed{0.5}$ (because $0.5 \times 0.5 = 0.25$)

2) $\sqrt{0.0001} = \boxed{0.01}$ (because $0.01 \times 0.01 = 0.0001$)

3) $\sqrt{0.81} = \boxed{0.9}$ (because $0.9 \times 0.9 = 0.81$)

4) $\sqrt{0.0004} = \boxed{0.02}$ (because $0.02 \times 0.02 = 0.0004$)

5) $\sqrt{1.44} = \boxed{1.2}$ (because $1.2 \times 1.2 = 1.44$)

6) $\sqrt{0.0036} = \boxed{0.06}$ (because $0.06 \times 0.06 = 0.0036$)

7) $\sqrt{0.0225} = \boxed{0.15}$ (because $0.15 \times 0.15 = 0.0225$)

8) $\sqrt{0.64} = \boxed{0.8}$ (because $0.8 \times 0.8 = 0.64$)

9) $\sqrt{0.000009} = \boxed{0.003}$ (because $0.003 \times 0.003 = 0.000009$)

10) $\sqrt{1.21} = \boxed{1.1}$ (because $1.1 \times 1.1 = 1.21$)

11) $\sqrt{0.000625} = \boxed{0.025}$ (because $0.025 \times 0.025 = 0.000625$)

12) $\sqrt{0.00000001} = \boxed{0.0001}$ (because $0.0001 \times 0.0001 = 0.00000001$)

Answer Key

Exercise Set 4.13

1) $7 \times (5.3 - 1.6) = 7 \times 3.7 = \boxed{25.9}$

2) $8.3 - 0.2 \times 4.9 = 8.3 - 0.98 = \boxed{7.32}$

3) $1.8^2 + 0.9^2 = 3.24 + 0.81 = \boxed{4.05}$

4) $(0.5 + 0.36) \times (2 - 0.7) = 0.86 \times 1.3 = \boxed{1.118}$

Note: You should perform the individual calculations like we did in Chapter 3 and in Sec.'s 4.1-4.12 (for example, by stacking the numbers vertically to add, subtract, or multiply).

5) $0.6 \times 0.45 - 0.9 \times (0.04 + 0.08) = 0.27 - 0.9 \times 0.12 = 0.27 - 0.108 = \boxed{0.162}$

6) $1.3 + 0.7 \times 0.2 + 0.8 = 1.3 + 0.14 + 0.8 = 1.44 + 0.8 = \boxed{2.24}$

7) $0.4^2 - 0.05 \times 1.7 = 0.16 - 0.085 = \boxed{0.075}$

8) $(7 \times 0.4 - 0.9)^2 = (2.8 - 0.9)^2 = 1.9^2 = \boxed{3.61}$

Exercise Set 4.14

1) $578 = 5.78 \times 10^2$

2) $0.067 = 6.7 \times 10^{-2}$

3) $0.000268 = 2.68 \times 10^{-4}$

4) $35,200 = 3.52 \times 10^4$

5) $0.004276 = 4.276 \times 10^{-3}$

6) $145.54 = 1.4554 \times 10^2$

7) $786,000 = 7.86 \times 10^5$

8) $0.00000964 = 9.64 \times 10^{-6}$

9) $0.32 = 3.2 \times 10^{-1}$

10) $7689.2 = 7.6892 \times 10^3$

11) $1,400,000 = 1.4 \times 10^6$

12) $0.0005 = 5 \times 10^{-4}$

13) $0.088 = 8.8 \times 10^{-2}$

14) $42,300 = 4.23 \times 10^4$

15) $365,400,000 = 3.654 \times 10^8$

16) $0.000000096 = 9.6 \times 10^{-8}$

17) $0.0000421 = 4.21 \times 10^{-5}$

18) $23,000,000 = 2.3 \times 10^7$

Chapter 5 Divide Decimals

Exercise Set 5.1

1) $38.9 \div 100 = 0.389$ (shift the decimal point 2 places to the left)
2) $0.0096 \div 0.01 = 0.96$ (shift the decimal point 2 places to the right)
3) $7.2 \div 10 = 0.72$ (shift the decimal point 1 place to the left)
4) $0.16 \div 0.001 = 160$ (shift the decimal point 3 places to the right)
5) $0.028 \div 0.0001 = 280$ (shift the decimal point 4 places to the right)
6) $0.47 \div 100 = 0.0047$ (shift the decimal point 2 places to the left)
7) $8.6 \div 0.1 = 86$ (shift the decimal point 1 place to the right)
8) $0.496 \div 1000 = 0.000496$ (shift the decimal point 3 places to the left)
9) $0.00101 \div 10,000 = 0.000000101$ (shift the decimal point 4 places to the left)
10) $25.4 \div 0.01 = 2540$ (shift the decimal point 2 places to the right)
11) $0.052 \div 100 = 0.00052$ (shift the decimal point 2 places to the left)
12) $9.74 \div 0.00001 = 974,000$ (shift the decimal point 5 places to the right)
13) $3.5 \div 0.001 = 3500$ (shift the decimal point 3 places to the right)
14) $473 \div 100,000 = 0.00473$ (shift the decimal point 5 places to the left)
15) $96.7 \div 1000 = 0.0967$ (shift the decimal point 3 places to the left)
16) $0.0793 \div 0.1 = 0.793$ (shift the decimal point 1 place to the right)
17) $0.0063 \div 0.000001 = 6300$ (shift the decimal point 6 places to the right)
18) $5400 \div 1,000,000 = 0.0054$ (shift the decimal point 6 places to the left)
19) $0.75 \div 0.01 = 75$ (shift the decimal point 2 places to the right)
20) $0.00888 \div 0.0000001 = 88,800$ (shift the decimal point 7 places to the right)
21) $49,300 \div 10,000,000 = 0.00493$ (shift the decimal point 7 places to the left)
22) $0.042637 \div 0.001 = 42.637$ (shift the decimal point 3 places to the right)
23) $4.15 \div 100 = 0.0415$ (shift the decimal point 2 places to the left)
24) $0.006 \div 0.00001 = 600$ (shift the decimal point 5 places to the right)

Answer Key

Exercise Set 5.2

1)
$$\begin{array}{r}0.73\\5\overline{)3.65}\\\underline{3.5}\\0.15\end{array}$$

2)
$$\begin{array}{r}0.46\\2\overline{)0.92}\\\underline{0.8}\\0.12\end{array}$$

3)
$$\begin{array}{r}6.3\\9\overline{)56.7}\\\underline{54}\\2.7\end{array}$$

4)
$$\begin{array}{r}0.234\\6\overline{)1.404}\\\underline{1.2}\\0.20\\\underline{0.18}\\0.024\end{array}$$

5)
$$\begin{array}{r}0.045\\4\overline{)0.180}\\\underline{0.16}\\0.020\end{array}$$

6)
$$\begin{array}{r}0.0091\\8\overline{)0.0728}\\\underline{0.072}\\0.0008\end{array}$$

7)
$$\begin{array}{r}2.8\\3\overline{)8.4}\\\underline{6}\\2.4\end{array}$$

8)
$$\begin{array}{r}0.0146\\7\overline{)0.1022}\\\underline{0.07}\\0.032\\\underline{0.028}\\0.0042\end{array}$$

9)
$$\begin{array}{r}8.7\\6\overline{)52.2}\\\underline{48}\\4.2\end{array}$$

10)
$$\begin{array}{r}0.637\\7\overline{)4.459}\\\underline{4.2}\\0.25\\\underline{0.21}\\0.049\end{array}$$

11)
$$\begin{array}{r}0.222\\5\overline{)1.110}\\\underline{1.0}\\0.11\\\underline{0.10}\\0.010\end{array}$$

12)
$$\begin{array}{r}0.375\\2\overline{)0.750}\\\underline{0.6}\\0.15\\\underline{0.14}\\0.010\end{array}$$

13)
$$\begin{array}{r}0.094\\9\overline{)0.846}\\\underline{0.81}\\0.36\end{array}$$

14)
$$\begin{array}{r}0.0058\\3\overline{)0.0174}\\\underline{0.015}\\0.0024\end{array}$$

15)
$$\begin{array}{r}0.235\\8\overline{)1.880}\\\underline{1.6}\\0.28\\\underline{0.24}\\0.040\end{array}$$

16)
$$\begin{array}{r}0.613\\4\overline{)2.452}\\\underline{2.4}\\0.05\\\underline{0.04}\\0.012\end{array}$$

17)
$$\begin{array}{r}0.00035\\8\overline{)0.00280}\\\underline{0.0024}\\0.00040\end{array}$$

18)
$$\begin{array}{r}0.062\\5\overline{)0.310}\\\underline{0.30}\\0.010\end{array}$$

19)
$$\begin{array}{r}7.634\\2\overline{)15.268}\\\underline{14}\\1.2\\\underline{1.2}\\0.06\\\underline{0.06}\\0.008\end{array}$$

20)
$$\begin{array}{r}0.088\\6\overline{)0.528}\\\underline{0.48}\\0.048\end{array}$$

21)
$$\begin{array}{r}0.643\\7\overline{)4.501}\\\underline{4.2}\\0.30\\\underline{0.28}\\0.021\end{array}$$

22)
$$\begin{array}{r}0.0079\\3\overline{)0.0237}\\\underline{0.021}\\0.0027\end{array}$$

23)
$$\begin{array}{r}0.0625\\4\overline{)0.2500}\\\underline{0.24}\\0.010\\\underline{0.008}\\0.0020\end{array}$$

24)
$$\begin{array}{r}0.00143\\9\overline{)0.01287}\\\underline{0.009}\\0.0038\\\underline{0.0036}\\0.00027\end{array}$$

Exercise Set 5.3

1)
$$\begin{array}{r}0.42\\36\overline{)15.12}\\\underline{14.4}\\0.72\end{array}$$

2)
$$\begin{array}{r}0.07\\54\overline{)3.78}\end{array}$$

3)
$$\begin{array}{r}6.3\\72\overline{)453.6}\\\underline{432}\\21.6\end{array}$$

4)
$$\begin{array}{r}0.0065\\18\overline{)0.1170}\\\underline{0.108}\\0.0090\end{array}$$

5)
$$\begin{array}{r}0.3\\61\overline{)18.3}\end{array}$$

6)
$$\begin{array}{r}0.712\\49\overline{)34.888}\\\underline{34.3}\\0.58\\\underline{0.49}\\0.098\end{array}$$

7)
$$\begin{array}{r}0.025\\27\overline{)0.675}\\\underline{0.54}\\0.135\end{array}$$

8)
$$\begin{array}{r}0.004\\93\overline{)0.372}\end{array}$$

Answer Key

9)
```
        8.1
55)445.5
    440
     5.5
```

10)
```
      0.485
80)38.800
   32.0
    6.80
    6.40
    0.400
```

11)
```
      1.7
34)57.8
   34
   23.8
```

12)
```
      0.096
62)5.952
   5.58
   0.372
```

13)
```
      0.64
13)8.32
   7.8
   0.52
```

14)
```
       0.0725
28)2.0300
   1.96
   0.070
   0.056
   0.0140
```

15)
```
       0.0083
41)0.3403
   0.328
   0.0123
```

16)
```
       4.26
76)323.76
   304
    19.7
    15.2
     4.56
```

Exercise Set 5.4

1) $2.24 \div 7 = 0.32$

Note: We have only drawn the final answer.

2) $6.15 \div 5 = 1.23$

3) $3.2 \div 8 = 0.4$

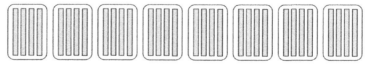

Exercise Set 5.5

1) $0.12 \div 0.4 = 0.3$ (since $0.4 \times 0.3 = 0.12$)
2) $1.6 \div 0.2 = 8$ (since $0.2 \times 8 = 1.6$)
3) $0.025 \div 0.5 = 0.05$ (since $0.5 \times 0.05 = 0.025$)
4) $0.28 \div 0.04 = 7$ (since $0.04 \times 7 = 0.28$)
5) $3.6 \div 9 = 0.4$ (since $9 \times 0.4 = 3.6$)
6) $0.01 \div 0.05 = 0.2$ (since $0.05 \times 0.2 = 0.010 = 0.01$)
7) $0.006 \div 0.002 = 3$ (since $0.002 \times 3 = 0.006$)
8) $0.32 \div 40 = 0.008$ (since $40 \times 0.008 = 0.32$)
9) $81 \div 900 = 0.09$ (since $900 \times 0.09 = 81$)
10) $0.024 \div 0.4 = 0.06$ (since $0.4 \times 0.06 = 0.024$)
11) $0.21 \div 0.03 = 7$ (since $0.03 \times 7 = 0.21$)
12) $0.2 \div 0.4 = 0.5$ (since $0.4 \times 0.5 = 0.20 = 0.2$)
13) $0.4 \div 0.2 = 2$ (since $0.2 \times 2 = 0.4$)
14) $0.072 \div 0.9 = 0.08$ (since $0.9 \times 0.08 = 0.072$)
15) $4.8 \div 6 = 0.8$ (since $6 \times 0.8 = 4.8$)
16) $0.0032 \div 0.8 = 0.004$ (since $0.8 \times 0.004 = 0.0032$)
17) $0.005 \div 0.01 = 0.5$ (since $0.01 \times 0.5 = 0.005$)
18) $0.42 \div 0.007 = 60$ (since $0.007 \times 60 = 0.420 = 0.42$)
19) $4.5 \div 5 = 0.9$ (since $5 \times 0.9 = 4.5$)
20) $0.027 \div 0.0009 = 30$ (since $0.0009 \times 30 = 0.0270 = 0.027$)
21) $0.64 \div 0.8 = 0.8$ (since $0.8 \times 0.8 = 0.64$)
22) $0.06 \div 0.02 = 3$ (since $0.02 \times 3 = 0.06$)
23) $0.0054 \div 0.006 = 0.9$ (since $0.006 \times 0.9 = 0.0054$)
24) $24 \div 0.3 = 80$ (since $0.3 \times 80 = 24$)
25) $0.28 \div 0.04 = 7$ (since $0.04 \times 7 = 0.28$)
26) $0.16 \div 8 = 0.02$ (since $8 \times 0.02 = 0.16$)
27) $0.00056 \div 0.7 = 0.0008$ (since $0.7 \times 0.0008 = 0.00056$)
28) $0.02 \div 0.05 = 0.4$ (since $0.05 \times 0.4 = 0.020 = 0.02$)
29) $0.045 \div 0.09 = 0.5$ (since $0.09 \times 0.5 = 0.045$)
30) $0.12 \div 2 = 0.06$ (since $2 \times 0.06 = 0.12$)

Answer Key

31) 0.36 ÷ 0.006 = 60 (since 0.006 × 60 = 0.360 = 0.36)

32) 72 ÷ 0.008 = 9000 (since 0.008 × 9000 = 72.000 = 72)

Exercise Set 5.6

1)
$$\begin{array}{r} 0.76 \\ 0.4\overline{)0.304} \\ \underline{0.28} \\ 0.024 \end{array}$$

2)
$$\begin{array}{r} 8.2 \\ 0.6\overline{)4.92} \\ \underline{4.8} \\ 0.12 \end{array}$$

3)
$$\begin{array}{r} 0.16 \\ 0.03\overline{)0.0048} \\ \underline{0.003} \\ 0.0018 \end{array}$$

4)
$$\begin{array}{r} 0.025 \\ 0.7\overline{)0.0175} \\ \underline{0.014} \\ 0.0035 \end{array}$$

5)
$$\begin{array}{r} 9.2 \\ 0.05\overline{)0.460} \\ \underline{0.45} \\ 0.010 \end{array}$$

6)
$$\begin{array}{r} 38.1 \\ 0.2\overline{)7.62} \\ \underline{6} \\ 1.6 \\ \underline{1.6} \\ 0.02 \end{array}$$

7)
$$\begin{array}{r} 84 \\ 0.009\overline{)0.756} \\ \underline{0.72} \\ 0.036 \end{array}$$

8)
$$\begin{array}{r} 0.00038 \\ 0.1\overline{)0.000038} \\ \underline{0.00003} \\ 0.000008 \end{array}$$

9)
$$\begin{array}{r} 62 \\ 0.8\overline{)49.6} \\ \underline{48} \\ 1.6 \end{array}$$

10)
$$\begin{array}{r} 0.95 \\ 0.07\overline{)0.0665} \\ \underline{0.063} \\ 0.0035 \end{array}$$

11)
$$\begin{array}{r} 0.67 \\ 0.6\overline{)0.402} \\ \underline{0.36} \\ 0.042 \end{array}$$

12)
$$\begin{array}{r} 364 \\ 0.05\overline{)18.20} \\ \underline{15} \\ 3.2 \\ \underline{3.0} \\ 0.20 \end{array}$$

13)
$$\begin{array}{r} 71 \\ 0.009\overline{)0.639} \\ \underline{0.63} \\ 0.009 \end{array}$$

14)
$$\begin{array}{r} 3.03 \\ 0.1\overline{)0.303} \\ \underline{0.3} \\ 0.00 \\ \underline{0.00} \\ 0.003 \end{array}$$

15)
$$\begin{array}{r} 27 \\ 0.08\overline{)2.16} \\ \underline{1.6} \\ 0.56 \end{array}$$

16)
$$\begin{array}{r} 0.992 \\ 0.2\overline{)0.1984} \\ \underline{0.18} \\ 0.018 \\ \underline{0.018} \\ 0.0004 \end{array}$$

17)
$$\begin{array}{r} 2.18 \\ 0.03 \overline{)0.0654} \\ \underline{0.06} \\ 0.005 \\ \underline{0.003} \\ 0.0024 \end{array}$$

18)
$$\begin{array}{r} 0.079 \\ 0.6 \overline{)0.0474} \\ \underline{0.042} \\ 0.0054 \end{array}$$

19)
$$\begin{array}{r} 0.85 \\ 0.4 \overline{)0.340} \\ \underline{0.32} \\ 0.020 \end{array}$$

20)
$$\begin{array}{r} 1852 \\ 0.07 \overline{)129.64} \\ \underline{70} \\ 59 \\ \underline{56} \\ 3.6 \\ \underline{3.5} \\ 0.14 \end{array}$$

21)
$$\begin{array}{r} 0.0088 \\ 0.2 \overline{)0.00176} \\ \underline{0.0016} \\ 0.00016 \end{array}$$

22)
$$\begin{array}{r} 61.6 \\ 0.05 \overline{)3.080} \\ \underline{3.0} \\ 0.08 \\ \underline{0.05} \\ 0.030 \end{array}$$

23)
$$\begin{array}{r} 0.604 \\ 0.9 \overline{)0.5436} \\ \underline{0.54} \\ 0.003 \\ \underline{0.000} \\ 0.0036 \end{array}$$

24)
$$\begin{array}{r} 42.7 \\ 0.001 \overline{)0.0427} \\ \underline{0.04} \\ 0.002 \\ \underline{0.002} \\ 0.0007 \end{array}$$

25)
$$\begin{array}{r} 29.6 \\ 0.07 \overline{)2.072} \\ \underline{1.4} \\ 0.67 \\ \underline{0.63} \\ 0.042 \end{array}$$

26)
$$\begin{array}{r} 0.053 \\ 0.4 \overline{)0.0212} \\ \underline{0.020} \\ 0.0012 \end{array}$$

27)
$$\begin{array}{r} 16.49 \\ 0.06 \overline{)0.9894} \\ \underline{0.6} \\ 0.38 \\ \underline{0.36} \\ 0.029 \\ \underline{0.024} \\ 0.0054 \end{array}$$

28)
$$\begin{array}{r} 0.00046 \\ 0.8 \overline{)0.000368} \\ \underline{0.00032} \\ 0.000048 \end{array}$$

Exercise Set 5.7

1)
$$\begin{array}{r} 0.72 \\ 0.36 \overline{)0.2592} \\ \underline{0.252} \\ 0.0072 \end{array}$$

2)
$$\begin{array}{r} 0.019 \\ 7.2 \overline{)0.1368} \\ \underline{0.072} \\ 0.0648 \end{array}$$

3)
$$\begin{array}{r} 8 \\ 0.049 \overline{)0.392} \end{array}$$

4)
$$\begin{array}{r} 0.64 \\ 0.83 \overline{)0.5312} \\ \underline{0.498} \\ 0.0332 \end{array}$$

Answer Key

5)
$$\begin{array}{r}3.85\\5.4{\overline{\smash{\big)}\,20.790}}\\\underline{16.2}\\4.59\\\underline{4.32}\\0.270\end{array}$$

6)
$$\begin{array}{r}53\\0.018{\overline{\smash{\big)}\,0.954}}\\\underline{0.90}\\0.054\end{array}$$

7)
$$\begin{array}{r}4.7\\0.91{\overline{\smash{\big)}\,4.277}}\\\underline{3.64}\\0.637\end{array}$$

8)
$$\begin{array}{r}80\\0.0027{\overline{\smash{\big)}\,0.216}}\end{array}$$

9)
$$\begin{array}{r}3.8\\0.065{\overline{\smash{\big)}\,0.2470}}\\\underline{0.195}\\0.0520\end{array}$$

10)
$$\begin{array}{r}0.055\\0.26{\overline{\smash{\big)}\,0.01430}}\\\underline{0.0130}\\0.00130\end{array}$$

11)
$$\begin{array}{r}0.0023\\8.8{\overline{\smash{\big)}\,0.02024}}\\\underline{0.0176}\\0.00264\end{array}$$

12)
$$\begin{array}{r}8.7\\0.052{\overline{\smash{\big)}\,0.4524}}\\\underline{0.416}\\0.0364\end{array}$$

13)
$$\begin{array}{r}16.4\\0.49{\overline{\smash{\big)}\,8.036}}\\\underline{4.9}\\3.13\\\underline{2.94}\\0.196\end{array}$$

14)
$$\begin{array}{r}3.5\\5.8{\overline{\smash{\big)}\,20.30}}\\\underline{17.4}\\2.90\end{array}$$

15)
$$\begin{array}{r}68.4\\0.075{\overline{\smash{\big)}\,5.1300}}\\\underline{4.5}\\0.63\\\underline{0.60}\\0.030\end{array}$$

16)
$$\begin{array}{r}45\\0.0094{\overline{\smash{\big)}\,0.4230}}\\\underline{0.376}\\0.0470\end{array}$$

Exercise Set 5.8

1)
$$\begin{array}{r}8.6\\5{\overline{\smash{\big)}\,43.0}}\\\underline{40}\\3.0\end{array}$$

2)
$$\begin{array}{r}2.75\\4{\overline{\smash{\big)}\,11.00}}\\\underline{8}\\3.0\\\underline{2.8}\\0.20\end{array}$$

3)
$$\begin{array}{r}3.5\\2{\overline{\smash{\big)}\,7.0}}\\\underline{6}\\1.0\end{array}$$

4)
$$\begin{array}{r}0.375\\8{\overline{\smash{\big)}\,3.000}}\\\underline{2.4}\\0.60\\\underline{0.56}\\0.040\end{array}$$

5)
$$\begin{array}{r}0.25\\4\overline{)1.00}\\\underline{0.8}\\0.20\end{array}$$

6)
$$\begin{array}{r}8.875\\8\overline{)71.000}\\\underline{64}\\7.0\\\underline{6.4}\\0.60\\\underline{0.56}\\0.040\end{array}$$

7)
$$\begin{array}{r}0.8\\5\overline{)4.0}\end{array}$$

8)
$$\begin{array}{r}0.5\\2\overline{)1.0}\end{array}$$

9)
$$\begin{array}{r}9.2\\5\overline{)46.0}\\\underline{45}\\1.0\end{array}$$

10)
$$\begin{array}{r}7.5\\2\overline{)15.0}\\\underline{14}\\1.0\end{array}$$

11)
$$\begin{array}{r}0.625\\8\overline{)5.000}\\\underline{4.8}\\0.20\\\underline{0.16}\\0.040\end{array}$$

12)
$$\begin{array}{r}2.5\\4\overline{)10.0}\\\underline{8}\\2.0\end{array}$$

13)
$$\begin{array}{r}0.125\\8\overline{)1.000}\\\underline{0.8}\\0.20\\\underline{0.16}\\0.040\end{array}$$

14)
$$\begin{array}{r}125.25\\4\overline{)501.00}\\\underline{4}\\10\\\underline{8}\\21\\\underline{20}\\1.0\\\underline{0.8}\\0.20\end{array}$$

15)
$$\begin{array}{r}12.5\\8\overline{)100.0}\\\underline{8}\\20\\\underline{16}\\4.0\end{array}$$

16)
$$\begin{array}{r}0.4\\5\overline{)2.0}\end{array}$$

Answer Key

17)
$$\begin{array}{r} 3.7 \\ 10\overline{)37.0} \\ \underline{30} \\ 7.0 \end{array}$$

18)
$$\begin{array}{r} 1.6 \\ 25\overline{)40.0} \\ \underline{25} \\ 15.0 \end{array}$$

19)
$$\begin{array}{r} 0.5625 \\ 16\overline{)9.0000} \\ \underline{8.0} \\ 1.00 \\ \underline{0.96} \\ 0.040 \\ \underline{0.032} \\ 0.0080 \end{array}$$

20)
$$\begin{array}{r} 7.5 \\ 40\overline{)300.0} \\ \underline{280} \\ 20.0 \end{array}$$

21)
$$\begin{array}{r} 0.2 \\ 20\overline{)4.0} \end{array}$$

22)
$$\begin{array}{r} 0.75 \\ 32\overline{)24.00} \\ \underline{22.4} \\ 1.60 \end{array}$$

23)
$$\begin{array}{r} 2.3 \\ 50\overline{)115.0} \\ \underline{100} \\ 15.0 \end{array}$$

24)
$$\begin{array}{r} 40.4 \\ 25\overline{)1010.0} \\ \underline{100} \\ 10 \\ \underline{0} \\ 10.0 \end{array}$$

25)
$$\begin{array}{r} 7.5 \\ 80\overline{)600.0} \\ \underline{560} \\ 40.0 \end{array}$$

26)
$$\begin{array}{r} 0.6875 \\ 16\overline{)11.0000} \\ \underline{9.6} \\ 1.40 \\ \underline{1.28} \\ 0.120 \\ \underline{0.112} \\ 0.0080 \end{array}$$

27)
$$\begin{array}{r} 2.8 \\ 250\overline{)700.0} \\ \underline{500} \\ 200.0 \end{array}$$

28)
$$\begin{array}{r} 0.6 \\ 125\overline{)75.0} \end{array}$$

Exercise Set 5.9

1) $\$4.95 \div 3 = \boxed{\$1.65}$

Note: You should perform the division like we have in the earlier sections of this chapter, meaning that you should show more work than we have shown here.

2) $6.84 \div 12 = \boxed{0.57}$ ounces

3) $r = \frac{d}{t} = 2.4 \div 0.5 = \boxed{4.8}$ mph (miles per hour)

4) Step 1: To find one-sixth of $108, divide $108 by six: $108 ÷ 6 = $18
Step 2: Subtract $18 from $108 to find the current total: $108 − $18 = $90
Step 3: To find one-fourth of $90, divide $90 by four: $90 ÷ 4 = $22.50
Step 4: Subtract $22.50 from $90 to find the current total: $90 − $22.50 = $67.50
Step 5: To find one-fifth of $67.50, divide $67.50 by five: $67.50 ÷ 5 = $13.50
Step 6: Subtract $13.50 from $67.50 to find the current total: $67.50 − $13.50 = $\boxed{\$54}$

5) Step 1: 8 × 145 = 1160 pounds
Step 2: 1500 − 1160 = 340 pounds
Step 3: 340 ÷ 80 = 4.25 kids
Since the number of kids must be a whole number, only $\boxed{4}$ kids can ride the elevator with the adults.

Exercise Set 5.10

1) $\frac{0.37+0.41}{2} = \frac{0.78}{2} = 0.39$

2) $\frac{5.8+5.93+6}{3} = \frac{17.73}{3} = 5.91$

3) $\frac{0.074+0.074+0.077+0.077+0.077}{5} = \frac{0.379}{5} = 0.0758$

4) $\frac{1.234+1.423+1.342}{3} = \frac{3.999}{3} = 1.333$

5) $\frac{0.764+0.77+0.781+0.8}{4} = \frac{3.115}{4} = 0.77875$

6) $\frac{0.089+0.09+0.096+0.1+0.103+0.11}{6} = \frac{0.588}{6} = 0.098$

Exercise Set 5.11

1) $\boxed{0.255}$ is closer to 0.27 because 0.22 and 0.255 are both less than 0.27 and because 0.255 is greater than 0.22 (it is not useful to find the average for this problem)

2) $\frac{0.078+0.133}{2} = \frac{0.211}{2} = 0.1055$

$\boxed{0.133}$ is closer to 0.11 because 0.11 is greater than the average (0.1055)

3) $\frac{1.47+1.74}{2} = \frac{3.21}{2} = 1.605$

$\boxed{1.74}$ is closer to 1.608 because 1.608 is greater than the average (1.605)

Answer Key

4) $\frac{0.88+0.9}{2} = \frac{1.78}{2} = 0.89$

$\boxed{0.88}$ is closer to 0.888 because 0.888 is less than the average (0.89)

5) $\boxed{18.136}$ is closer to 18 because 18.136 and 18.2 are both more than 18 and because 18.136 is less than 18.2 (it is not useful to find the average for this problem)

6) $\frac{0.397+0.406}{2} = \frac{0.803}{2} = 0.4015$

$\boxed{0.397}$ is closer to 0.4 because 0.4 is less than the average (0.4015)

7) $\frac{0.0016+0.0032}{2} = \frac{0.0048}{2} = 0.0024$

$\boxed{0.0016}$ is closer to 0.00239 because 0.00239 is less than the average (0.0024)

8) $\frac{6.238+6.328}{2} = \frac{12.566}{2} = 6.283$

$\boxed{6.328}$ is closer to 6.29 because 6.29 is greater than the average (6.283)

9) $\frac{0.066+0.091}{2} = \frac{0.157}{2} = 0.0785$

$\boxed{0.091}$ is closer to 0.079 because 0.079 is greater than the average (0.0785)

10) $\frac{0.00373+0.0151}{2} = \frac{0.01883}{2} = 0.009415$

$\boxed{0.0151}$ is closer to 0.00945 because 0.00945 is greater than the average (0.009415)

Chapter 6 Fractions and Decimals

Exercise Set 6.1

1)
$$\begin{array}{r} 0.5 \\ 2\overline{)1.0} \end{array}$$

2)
$$\begin{array}{r} 1.2 \\ 5\overline{)6.0} \\ \underline{5} \\ 1.0 \end{array}$$

3)
$$\begin{array}{r} 0.7 \\ 10\overline{)7.0} \end{array}$$

4)
$$\begin{array}{r} 0.25 \\ 4\overline{)1.00} \\ \underline{0.8} \\ 0.20 \end{array}$$

5)
$$\begin{array}{r} 2.8 \\ 5\overline{)14.0} \\ \underline{10} \\ 4.0 \end{array}$$

6)
$$\begin{array}{r} 0.875 \\ 8\overline{)7.000} \\ \underline{6.4} \\ 0.60 \\ \underline{0.56} \\ 0.040 \end{array}$$

7)
$$\begin{array}{r} 0.55 \\ 20\overline{)11.00} \\ \underline{10.0} \\ 1.00 \end{array}$$

8)
$$\begin{array}{r} 0.24 \\ 25\overline{)6.00} \\ \underline{5.0} \\ 1.00 \end{array}$$

9)
$$\begin{array}{r} 4.25 \\ 4\overline{)17.00} \\ \underline{16} \\ 1.0 \\ \underline{0.8} \\ 0.20 \end{array}$$

10)
$$\begin{array}{r} 1.375 \\ 8\overline{)11.000} \\ \underline{8} \\ 3.0 \\ \underline{2.4} \\ 0.60 \\ \underline{0.56} \\ 0.040 \end{array}$$

11)
$$\begin{array}{r} 0.34 \\ 50\overline{)17.00} \\ \underline{15.0} \\ 2.00 \end{array}$$

12)
$$\begin{array}{r} 9.5 \\ 2\overline{)19.0} \\ \underline{18} \\ 1.0 \end{array}$$

13)
$$\begin{array}{r} 5.6 \\ 5\overline{)28.0} \\ \underline{25} \\ 3.0 \end{array}$$

14)
$$\begin{array}{r} 7.75 \\ 4\overline{)31.00} \\ \underline{28} \\ 3.0 \\ \underline{2.8} \\ 0.20 \end{array}$$

15)
$$\begin{array}{r} 0.225 \\ 40\overline{)9.000} \\ \underline{8.0} \\ 1.00 \\ \underline{0.80} \\ 0.200 \end{array}$$

16)
$$\begin{array}{r} 0.3125 \\ 16\overline{)5.0000} \\ \underline{4.8} \\ 0.20 \\ \underline{0.16} \\ 0.040 \\ \underline{0.032} \\ 0.0080 \end{array}$$

Answer Key

Exercise Set 6.2

1) $\frac{3}{2} = \frac{3 \times 5}{2 \times 5} = \frac{15}{10} = 1.5$

2) $\frac{3}{5} = \frac{3 \times 2}{5 \times 2} = \frac{6}{10} = 0.6$

3) $\frac{7}{4} = \frac{7 \times 25}{4 \times 25} = \frac{175}{100} = 1.75$

4) $\frac{9}{10} = 0.9$

5) $\frac{17}{20} = \frac{17 \times 5}{20 \times 5} = \frac{85}{100} = 0.85$

6) $\frac{11}{25} = \frac{11 \times 4}{25 \times 4} = \frac{44}{100} = 0.44$

7) $\frac{49}{50} = \frac{49 \times 2}{50 \times 2} = \frac{98}{100} = 0.98$

8) $\frac{5}{8} = \frac{5 \times 125}{8 \times 125} = \frac{625}{1000} = 0.625$

9) $\frac{6}{5} = \frac{6 \times 2}{5 \times 2} = \frac{12}{10} = 1.2$

10) $\frac{4}{125} = \frac{4 \times 8}{125 \times 8} = \frac{32}{1000} = 0.032$

11) $\frac{63}{100} = 0.63$

12) $\frac{9}{40} = \frac{9 \times 25}{40 \times 25} = \frac{225}{1000} = 0.225$

13) $\frac{3}{8} = \frac{3 \times 125}{8 \times 125} = \frac{375}{1000} = 0.375$

14) $\frac{21}{4} = \frac{21 \times 25}{4 \times 25} = \frac{525}{100} = 5.25$

15) $\frac{41}{250} = \frac{41 \times 4}{250 \times 4} = \frac{164}{1000} = 0.164$

16) $\frac{16}{25} = \frac{16 \times 4}{25 \times 4} = \frac{64}{100} = 0.64$

17) $\frac{5}{16} = \frac{5 \times 625}{16 \times 625} = \frac{3125}{10,000} = 0.3125$

Exercise Set 6.3

1) $6\frac{1}{4} = 6 + \frac{1 \times 25}{4 \times 25} = 6 + \frac{25}{100} = 6.25$

2) $3\frac{1}{2} = 3 + \frac{1 \times 5}{2 \times 5} = 3 + \frac{5}{10} = 3.5$

3) $1\frac{3}{5} = 1 + \frac{3 \times 2}{5 \times 2} = 1 + \frac{6}{10} = 1.6$

4) $5\frac{1}{10} = 5 + \frac{1}{10} = 5.1$

5) $4\frac{7}{8} = 4 + \frac{7 \times 125}{8 \times 125} = 4 + \frac{875}{1000} = 4.875$

6) $9\frac{21}{50} = 9 + \frac{21 \times 2}{50 \times 2} = 9 + \frac{42}{100} = 9.42$

7) $7\frac{13}{20} = 7 + \frac{13 \times 5}{20 \times 5} = 7 + \frac{65}{100} = 7.65$ 8) $2\frac{49}{250} = 2 + \frac{49 \times 4}{250 \times 4} = 2 + \frac{196}{1000} = 2.196$

9) $26\frac{3}{100} = 26 + 0.03 = 26.03$

10) $47\frac{11}{80} = 47 + \frac{11 \times 125}{80 \times 125} = 47 + \frac{1375}{10,000} = 47.1375$

Exercise Set 6.4

1) $0.5 = \frac{5}{10} = \frac{5 \div 5}{10 \div 5} = \frac{1}{2}$ 2) $1.25 = \frac{125}{100} = \frac{125 \div 25}{100 \div 25} = \frac{5}{4}$

3) $0.625 = \frac{625}{1000} = \frac{625 \div 125}{1000 \div 125} = \frac{5}{8}$ 4) $0.4 = \frac{4}{10} = \frac{4 \div 2}{10 \div 2} = \frac{2}{5}$

5) $1.68 = \frac{168}{100} = \frac{168 \div 4}{100 \div 4} = \frac{42}{25}$ 6) $0.775 = \frac{775}{1000} = \frac{775 \div 25}{1000 \div 25} = \frac{31}{40}$

7) $5.5 = \frac{55}{10} = \frac{55 \div 5}{10 \div 5} = \frac{11}{2}$ 8) $0.08 = \frac{8}{100} = \frac{8 \div 4}{100 \div 4} = \frac{2}{25}$

9) $1.52 = \frac{152}{100} = \frac{152 \div 4}{100 \div 4} = \frac{38}{25}$ 10) $10.1 = \frac{101}{10}$

11) $1.375 = \frac{1375}{1000} = \frac{1375 \div 125}{1000 \div 125} = \frac{11}{8}$ 12) $2.25 = \frac{225}{100} = \frac{225 \div 25}{100 \div 25} = \frac{9}{4}$

13) $0.2 = \frac{2}{10} = \frac{2 \div 2}{10 \div 2} = \frac{1}{5}$ 14) $0.048 = \frac{48}{1000} = \frac{48 \div 8}{1000 \div 8} = \frac{6}{125}$

15) $0.86 = \frac{86}{100} = \frac{86 \div 2}{100 \div 2} = \frac{43}{50}$ 16) $3.2 = \frac{32}{10} = \frac{32 \div 2}{10 \div 2} = \frac{16}{5}$

17) $1.736 = \frac{1736}{1000} = \frac{1736 \div 8}{1000 \div 8} = \frac{217}{125}$ 18) $0.35 = \frac{35}{100} = \frac{35 \div 5}{100 \div 5} = \frac{7}{20}$

19) $2.5 = \frac{25}{10} = \frac{25 \div 5}{10 \div 5} = \frac{5}{2}$ 20) $0.272 = \frac{272}{1000} = \frac{272 \div 8}{1000 \div 8} = \frac{34}{125}$

Exercise Set 6.5

1) $4.25 = 4 + \frac{25 \div 25}{100 \div 25} = 4\frac{1}{4}$ 2) $6.5 = 6 + \frac{5 \div 5}{10 \div 5} = 6\frac{1}{2}$

3) $3.8 = 3 + \frac{8 \div 2}{10 \div 2} = 3\frac{4}{5}$ 4) $2.049 = 2 + \frac{49}{1000} = 2\frac{49}{1000}$

5) $1.5 = 1 + \frac{5 \div 5}{10 \div 5} = 1\frac{1}{2}$ 6) $8.75 = 8 + \frac{75 \div 25}{100 \div 25} = 8\frac{3}{4}$

7) $3.125 = 3 + \frac{125 \div 125}{1000 \div 125} = 3\frac{1}{8}$ 8) $5.2 = 5 + \frac{2 \div 2}{10 \div 2} = 5\frac{1}{5}$

9) $2.4 = 2 + \frac{4 \div 2}{10 \div 2} = 2\frac{2}{5}$ 10) $4.066 = 4 + \frac{66 \div 2}{1000 \div 2} = 4\frac{33}{500}$

11) $9.25 = 9 + \frac{25 \div 25}{100 \div 25} = 9\frac{1}{4}$ 12) $7.16 = 7 + \frac{16 \div 4}{100 \div 4} = 7\frac{4}{25}$

Answer Key

13) $6.1 = 6 + \frac{1}{10} = 6\frac{1}{10}$

14) $1.6 = 1 + \frac{6 \div 2}{10 \div 2} = 1\frac{3}{5}$

15) $4.375 = 4 + \frac{375 \div 125}{1000 \div 125} = 4\frac{3}{8}$

16) $3.92 = 3 + \frac{92 \div 4}{100 \div 4} = 3\frac{23}{25}$

17) $8.54 = 8 + \frac{54 \div 2}{100 \div 2} = 8\frac{27}{50}$

18) $2.136 = 2 + \frac{136 \div 8}{1000 \div 8} = 2\frac{17}{125}$

19) $7.8 = 7 + \frac{8 \div 2}{10 \div 2} = 7\frac{4}{5}$

20) $16.45 = 16 + \frac{45 \div 5}{100 \div 5} = 16\frac{9}{20}$

Exercise Set 6.6

1) Step 1: $t = \frac{3}{4} = \frac{3 \times 25}{4 \times 25} = \frac{75}{100} = 0.75$ hr

Step 2: $r = \frac{d}{t} = \frac{5.4}{0.75} = 5.4 \div 0.75 = \boxed{7.2}$ mph (miles per hour)

Note: You should perform the arithmetic like we did in Chapters 3-5, meaning that you should show more work than we have shown here.

2) Step 1: $\frac{7}{10} = 0.7$ feet. Step 2: $3.24 - 0.7 = \boxed{2.54}$ feet

3) Step 1: $\frac{2}{5} = \frac{2 \times 2}{5 \times 2} = \frac{4}{10} = 0.4$. Step 2: $\$8.25 \times 0.4 = \boxed{\$3.30}$

4) Step 1: $2\frac{3}{5} = 2 + \frac{3}{5} = 2 + \frac{3 \times 2}{5 \times 2} = 2 + \frac{6}{10} = 2 + 0.6 = 2.6$. Step 2: $2.26 \times 2.6 = \boxed{5.876}$ kilograms

5) Step 1: $\frac{5}{8} = \frac{5 \times 125}{8 \times 125} = \frac{625}{1000} = 0.625$ hours. Step 2: $1.6 - 0.625 = \boxed{0.975}$ hours

Exercise Set 6.7

1) $0.62 > \frac{3}{5}$ (since $\frac{3 \times 2}{5 \times 2} = \frac{6}{10} = 0.6$)

2) $\frac{5}{2} > 2.47$ (since $\frac{5 \times 5}{2 \times 5} = \frac{25}{10} = 2.5$)

3) $\frac{13}{4} < 3.5$ (since $\frac{13 \times 25}{4 \times 25} = \frac{325}{100} = 3.25$)

4) $0.85 = \frac{17}{20}$ (since $\frac{17 \times 5}{20 \times 5} = \frac{85}{100} = 0.85$)

5) $0.15 < \frac{21}{125}$ (since $\frac{21 \times 8}{125 \times 8} = \frac{168}{1000} = 0.168$)

6) $1.4 > \frac{67}{50}$ (since $\frac{67 \times 2}{50 \times 2} = \frac{134}{100} = 1.34$)

7) $0.048 < \frac{1}{20}$ (since $\frac{1 \times 5}{20 \times 5} = \frac{5}{100} = 0.05$)

8) $\frac{7}{8} < 0.88$ (since $\frac{7 \times 125}{8 \times 125} = \frac{875}{1000} = 0.875$)

9) $\frac{3}{16} > 0.187$ (since $\frac{3 \times 625}{16 \times 625} = \frac{1875}{10,000} = 0.1875$)

10) $0.225 = \frac{9}{40}$ (since $\frac{9 \times 25}{40 \times 25} = \frac{225}{1000} = 0.225$)

Chapter 7 Repeating Decimals

Exercise Set 7.1

1) $0.\overline{2} = 22222222...$
2) $0.\overline{49} = 0.49494949...$
3) $0.\overline{861} = 0.861861861861...$
4) $0.5\overline{3} = 0.533333333...$
5) $0.24\overline{76} = 0.2476767676...$
6) $0.\overline{7} = 0.77777777...$
7) $0.\overline{03} = 0.03030303...$
8) $0.\overline{30} = 0.30303030...$
9) $0.0\overline{3} = 0.03333333...$
10) $2.\overline{1} = 2.11111111...$
11) $0.\overline{655} = 0.655655655655...$
12) $0.\overline{565} = 0.565565565565...$
13) $0.\overline{556} = 0.556556556556...$
14) $0.\overline{009} = 0.009009009009...$
15) $0.\overline{090} = 0.090090090090...$
16) $0.\overline{900} = 0.900900900900...$
17) $5.3\overline{48} = 5.348484848...$
18) $0.002\overline{898} = 0.00289828982898...$
19) $1.23\overline{456789} = 1.234567895678956789...$
20) $0.\overline{4114} = 0.411441144114...$
21) $0.88888888... = 0.\overline{8}$
22) $5.2525252... = 5.\overline{25}$
23) $0.747274727472... = 0.\overline{7472}$
24) $1.99999999... = 1.\overline{9}$
25) $0.428571428571... = 0.\overline{428571}$
26) $16.32846846846... = 16.32\overline{846}$
27) $0.5677777777... = 0.56\overline{7}$
28) $0.1867867867867... = 0.1\overline{867}$
29) $1.034343434... = 1.0\overline{34}$
30) $763.2323232... = 763.\overline{23}$
31) $0.00021212121... = 0.000\overline{21}$
32) $3.363363363363... = 3.\overline{363}$
33) $0.336336336336... = 0.\overline{336}$
34) $0.663663663663... = 0.\overline{663}$
35) $0.0022222222... = 0.00\overline{2}$
36) $0.010010010010... = 0.\overline{010}$

Note: $0.0\overline{100}$ is equivalent to $0.\overline{010}$ (though $0.\overline{010}$ is preferable).

37) $0.100100100100... = 0.\overline{100}$
38) $8.80880880880... = 8.\overline{808}$
39) $0.0060606060... = 0.0\overline{06}$
40) $0.22255555555... = 0.222\overline{5}$

Note: $0.00\overline{60}$ is equivalent to $0.0\overline{06}$ (though $0.0\overline{06}$ is preferable).

Answer Key

Exercise Set 7.2

1) $0.44...$
    $9\overline{)4.000}$
    $\underline{3.6}$
    0.40
    $\underline{0.36}$
    0.040

    $\dfrac{4}{9} = 0.\overline{4}$

2) $0.66...$
    $3\overline{)2.000}$
    $\underline{1.8}$
    0.20
    $\underline{0.18}$
    0.020

    $\dfrac{2}{3} = 0.\overline{6}$

Note: You can also check these answers using a calculator.

3) $0.7272...$
    $11\overline{)8.00000}$
    $\underline{7.7}$
    0.30
    $\underline{0.22}$
    0.080
    $\underline{0.077}$
    0.0030
    $\underline{0.0022}$
    0.00080

    $\dfrac{8}{11} = 0.\overline{72}$

4) $1.1...$
    $9\overline{)10.000}$
    $\underline{9}$
    0.10
    $\underline{0.09}$
    0.010

    $\dfrac{10}{9} = 1.\overline{1}$

5) $0.166...$
    $6\overline{)1.0000}$
    $\underline{0.6}$
    0.40
    $\underline{0.36}$
    0.040
    $\underline{0.036}$
    0.0040

    $\dfrac{1}{6} = 0.1\overline{6}$

6) $0.4166...$
    $12\overline{)5.00000}$
    $\underline{4.8}$
    0.20
    $\underline{0.12}$
    0.080
    $\underline{0.072}$
    0.0080
    $\underline{0.0072}$
    0.00080

    $\dfrac{5}{12} = 0.41\overline{6}$

7)
$$\begin{array}{r} 0.233... \\ 30\overline{)7.0000} \\ \underline{6.0} \\ 1.00 \\ \underline{0.90} \\ 0.100 \\ \underline{0.090} \\ 0.0100 \end{array}$$
$\dfrac{7}{30} = 0.2\overline{3}$

8)
$$\begin{array}{r} 0.7575... \\ 33\overline{)25.00000} \\ \underline{23.1} \\ 1.90 \\ \underline{1.65} \\ 0.250 \\ \underline{0.231} \\ 0.0190 \\ \underline{0.0165} \\ 0.00250 \end{array}$$
$\dfrac{25}{33} = 0.\overline{75}$

9)
$$\begin{array}{r} 4.5833... \\ 12\overline{)55.00000} \\ \underline{48} \\ 7.0 \\ \underline{6.0} \\ 1.00 \\ \underline{0.96} \\ 0.040 \\ \underline{0.036} \\ 0.0040 \\ \underline{0.0036} \\ 0.00040 \end{array}$$
$\dfrac{55}{12} = 4.58\overline{3}$

10)
$$\begin{array}{r} 0.266... \\ 15\overline{)4.0000} \\ \underline{3.0} \\ 1.00 \\ \underline{0.90} \\ 0.100 \\ \underline{0.090} \\ 0.0100 \end{array}$$
$\dfrac{4}{15} = 0.2\overline{6}$

Answer Key

11) 0.5656...
    99)$\overline{56.00000}$
    49.5
    6.50
    5.94
    0.560
    0.495
    0.0650
    0.0594
    0.00560

   $\dfrac{56}{99} = 0.\overline{56}$

12) 1.1388...
    36)$\overline{41.00000}$
    36
    5.0
    3.6
    1.40
    1.08
    0.320
    0.288
    0.0320
    0.0288
    0.00320

   $\dfrac{41}{36} = 1.13\overline{8}$

13) 0.611...
    18)$\overline{11.0000}$
    10.8
    0.20
    0.18
    0.020
    0.018
    0.0020

   $\dfrac{11}{18} = 0.6\overline{1}$

14) 0.71428571...
    7)$\overline{5.000000000}$
    4.9
    0.10
    0.07
    0.030
    0.028
    0.0020
    0.0014
    0.00060
    0.00056
    0.000040
    0.000035
    0.0000050
    0.0000049
    0.00000010
    0.00000007
    0.000000030

   $\dfrac{5}{7} = 0.\overline{714285}$

Exercise Set 7.3

1) $\frac{9}{70}$ is a reduced fraction and 70 has 7 as a prime factor: $2 \times 5 \times 7 = 70$.

Yes, $\frac{9}{70}$ forms a repeating decimal. Note that $\frac{9}{70} = 0.1\overline{285714}$.

2) $\frac{49}{1250}$ is a reduced fraction and 1250 can be formed exclusively by multiplying 2's and 5's together: $2 \times 5 \times 5 \times 5 \times 5 = 1250$.

No, $\frac{49}{1250}$ does **not** form a repeating decimal. Note that $\frac{49}{1250} = 0.0392$.

3) $\frac{63}{550}$ is a reduced fraction and 550 has 11 as a prime factor: $2 \times 5 \times 5 \times 11 = 550$.

Yes, $\frac{63}{550}$ forms a repeating decimal. Note that $\frac{63}{550} = 0.11\overline{45}$.

4) $\frac{11}{65}$ is a reduced fraction and 65 has 13 as a prime factor: $5 \times 13 = 65$.

Yes, $\frac{11}{65}$ forms a repeating decimal. Note that $\frac{11}{65} = 0.1\overline{692307}$.

5) $\frac{13}{65}$ can be reduced: $\frac{13}{65} = \frac{13 \div 13}{65 \div 13} = \frac{1}{5}$. The reduced fraction $\frac{1}{5}$ has a denominator of 5.

No, $\frac{13}{65}$ does **not** form a repeating decimal. Note that $\frac{13}{65} = 0.2$.

6) $\frac{99}{250}$ is a reduced fraction and 250 can be formed exclusively by multiplying 2's and 5's together: $2 \times 5 \times 5 \times 5 = 250$.

No, $\frac{99}{250}$ does **not** form a repeating decimal. Note that $\frac{99}{250} = 0.396$.

7) $\frac{25}{70}$ can be reduced: $\frac{25}{70} = \frac{25 \div 5}{70 \div 5} = \frac{5}{14}$. The denominator of the reduced fraction has 7 as a prime factor: $2 \times 7 = 14$.

Yes, $\frac{25}{70}$ forms a repeating decimal. Note that $\frac{25}{70} = 0.3\overline{571428}$.

8) $\frac{28}{70}$ can be reduced: $\frac{28}{70} = \frac{28 \div 14}{70 \div 14} = \frac{2}{5}$. The reduced fraction $\frac{2}{5}$ has a denominator of 5.

No, $\frac{28}{70}$ does **not** form a repeating decimal. Note that $\frac{28}{70} = 0.4$.

9) $\frac{189}{63}$ can be reduced: $\frac{189}{63} = \frac{189 \div 63}{63 \div 63} = \frac{3}{1} = 3$. This is a whole number (not a decimal).

No, $\frac{189}{63}$ does **not** form a repeating decimal. Note that $\frac{189}{63} = 189 \div 63 = 3$.

Answer Key

Exercise Set 7.4

1) $\frac{1}{3} = \frac{1 \times 3}{3 \times 3} = \frac{3}{9} = 0.\overline{3}$

2) $\frac{2}{9} = 0.\overline{2}$

3) $\frac{4}{11} = \frac{4 \times 9}{11 \times 9} = \frac{36}{99} = 0.\overline{36}$

4) $\frac{20}{33} = \frac{20 \times 3}{33 \times 3} = \frac{60}{99} = 0.\overline{60}$

Note: The 0 must be under the bar in $0.\overline{60}$.

5) $\frac{14}{333} = \frac{14 \times 3}{333 \times 3} = \frac{42}{999} = 0.\overline{042}$

6) $\frac{7}{111} = \frac{7 \times 9}{111 \times 9} = \frac{63}{999} = 0.\overline{063}$

Note: The 0 must be under the bar in $0.\overline{042}$ and $0.\overline{063}$.

7) $\frac{25}{27} = \frac{25 \times 37}{27 \times 37} = \frac{925}{999} = 0.\overline{925}$

8) $\frac{512}{3333} = \frac{512 \times 3}{3333 \times 3} = \frac{1536}{9999} = 0.\overline{1536}$

9) $\frac{36}{101} = \frac{36 \times 99}{101 \times 99} = \frac{3564}{9999} = 0.\overline{3564}$

10) $\frac{9}{37} = \frac{9 \times 27}{37 \times 27} = \frac{243}{999} = 0.\overline{243}$

11) $\frac{280}{333} = \frac{280 \times 3}{333 \times 3} = \frac{840}{999} = 0.\overline{840}$

12) $\frac{9}{11} = \frac{9 \times 9}{11 \times 9} = \frac{81}{99} = 0.\overline{81}$

Note: The 0 must be under the bar in $0.\overline{840}$.

13) $\frac{70}{99} = 0.\overline{70}$

14) $\frac{1}{111} = \frac{1 \times 9}{111 \times 9} = \frac{9}{999} = 0.\overline{009}$

Note: The 0's must be under the bar in $0.\overline{70}$ and $0.\overline{009}$.

15) $\frac{2}{33} = \frac{2 \times 3}{33 \times 3} = \frac{6}{99} = 0.\overline{06}$

16) $\frac{50}{999} = 0.\overline{050}$

Note: The 0's must be under the bar in $0.\overline{06}$ and $0.\overline{050}$.

17) $\frac{800}{1111} = \frac{800 \times 9}{1111 \times 9} = \frac{7200}{9999} = 0.\overline{7200}$

18) $\frac{31}{303} = \frac{31 \times 33}{303 \times 33} = \frac{1023}{9999} = 0.\overline{1023}$

Note: The 0's must be under the bar in $0.\overline{7200}$.

19) $\frac{9}{13} = \frac{9 \times 76{,}923}{13 \times 76{,}923} = \frac{692{,}307}{999{,}999} = 0.\overline{692307}$

20) $\frac{5}{271} = \frac{5 \times 369}{271 \times 369} = \frac{1845}{99{,}999} = 0.\overline{01845}$

Note: The 0 must be under the bar in $0.\overline{01845}$.

Exercise Set 7.5

1) $\frac{1}{30} = \frac{1 \times 3}{30 \times 3} = \frac{3}{90} = \frac{1}{10} \times \frac{3}{9} = \frac{1}{10} \times 0.\overline{3} = 0.0\overline{3}$

Note: None of the zeros are under the bar.

2) $\frac{1}{4500} = \frac{1 \times 2}{4500 \times 2} = \frac{2}{9000} = \frac{1}{1000} \times \frac{2}{9} = \frac{1}{1000} \times 0.\overline{2} = 0.000\overline{2}$

3) $\frac{49}{4950} = \frac{49 \times 2}{4950 \times 2} = \frac{98}{9900} = \frac{1}{100} \times \frac{98}{99} = \frac{1}{100} \times 0.\overline{98} = 0.00\overline{98}$

4) $\frac{1}{18} = \frac{1 \times 5}{18 \times 5} = \frac{5}{90} = \frac{1}{10} \times \frac{5}{9} = \frac{1}{10} \times 0.\overline{5} = 0.0\overline{5}$

5) $\dfrac{2}{225} = \dfrac{2 \times 4}{2 \times 225} = \dfrac{8}{900} = \dfrac{1}{100} \times \dfrac{8}{9} = \dfrac{1}{100} \times 0.\overline{8} = 0.00\overline{8}$

6) $\dfrac{29}{330} = \dfrac{29 \times 3}{330 \times 3} = \dfrac{87}{990} = \dfrac{1}{10} \times \dfrac{87}{99} = \dfrac{1}{10} \times 0.\overline{87} = 0.0\overline{87}$

7) $\dfrac{5}{198} = \dfrac{5 \times 5}{198 \times 5} = \dfrac{25}{990} = \dfrac{1}{10} \times \dfrac{25}{99} = \dfrac{1}{10} \times 0.\overline{25} = 0.0\overline{25}$

8) $\dfrac{2}{275} = \dfrac{2 \times 36}{275 \times 36} = \dfrac{72}{9900} = \dfrac{1}{100} \times \dfrac{72}{99} = \dfrac{1}{100} \times 0.\overline{72} = 0.00\overline{72}$

9) $\dfrac{83}{99{,}900} = \dfrac{1}{100} \times \dfrac{83}{999} = \dfrac{1}{100} \times 0.\overline{083} = 0.00\overline{083}$

Note: Only one of the 0's is under the bar in $0.00\overline{083}$.

10) $\dfrac{2}{45} = \dfrac{2 \times 2}{45 \times 2} = \dfrac{4}{90} = \dfrac{1}{10} \times \dfrac{4}{9} = \dfrac{1}{10} \times 0.\overline{4} = 0.0\overline{4}$

11) $\dfrac{1}{132} = \dfrac{1 \times 75}{132 \times 75} = \dfrac{75}{9900} = \dfrac{1}{100} \times \dfrac{75}{99} = \dfrac{1}{100} \times 0.\overline{75} = 0.00\overline{75}$

12) $\dfrac{4}{55} = \dfrac{4 \times 18}{55 \times 18} = \dfrac{72}{990} = \dfrac{1}{10} \times \dfrac{72}{99} = \dfrac{1}{10} \times 0.\overline{72} = 0.0\overline{72}$

13) $\dfrac{3}{1100} = \dfrac{3 \times 9}{1100 \times 9} = \dfrac{27}{9900} = \dfrac{1}{100} \times \dfrac{27}{99} = \dfrac{1}{100} \times 0.\overline{27} = 0.00\overline{27}$

14) $\dfrac{124}{4995} = \dfrac{124 \times 2}{4995 \times 2} = \dfrac{248}{9990} = \dfrac{1}{10} \times \dfrac{248}{999} = \dfrac{1}{10} \times 0.\overline{248} = 0.0\overline{248}$

15) $\dfrac{1}{1500} = \dfrac{1 \times 6}{1500 \times 6} = \dfrac{6}{9000} = \dfrac{1}{1000} \times \dfrac{6}{9} = \dfrac{1}{1000} \times 0.\overline{6} = 0.000\overline{6}$

16) $\dfrac{5}{66} = \dfrac{5 \times 15}{66 \times 15} = \dfrac{75}{990} = \dfrac{1}{10} \times \dfrac{75}{99} = \dfrac{1}{10} \times 0.\overline{75} = 0.0\overline{75}$

17) $\dfrac{1}{180} = \dfrac{1 \times 5}{180 \times 5} = \dfrac{5}{900} = \dfrac{1}{100} \times \dfrac{5}{9} = \dfrac{1}{100} \times 0.\overline{5} = 0.00\overline{5}$

18) $\dfrac{16}{2475} = \dfrac{16 \times 4}{2475 \times 4} = \dfrac{64}{9900} = \dfrac{1}{100} \times \dfrac{64}{99} = \dfrac{1}{100} \times 0.\overline{64} = 0.00\overline{64}$

Exercise Set 7.6

1) $\dfrac{4}{3} = \dfrac{3+1}{3} = \dfrac{3}{3} + \dfrac{1}{3} = 1 + \dfrac{1}{3} = 1 + \dfrac{1 \times 3}{3 \times 3} = 1 + \dfrac{3}{9} = 1 + 0.\overline{3} = 1.\overline{3}$

2) $\dfrac{5}{6} = \dfrac{5 \times 15}{6 \times 15} = \dfrac{75}{90} = \dfrac{1}{10} \times \dfrac{75}{9} = \dfrac{1}{10} \times \left(\dfrac{72+3}{9}\right) = \dfrac{1}{10} \times \left(\dfrac{72}{9} + \dfrac{3}{9}\right)$
$= \dfrac{1}{10} \times \left(8 + \dfrac{3}{9}\right) = \dfrac{1}{10} \times (8 + 0.\overline{3}) = \dfrac{1}{10} \times 8.\overline{3} = 0.8\overline{3}$ (only the 3 is under the bar)

3) $\dfrac{50}{33} = \dfrac{33+17}{33} = \dfrac{33}{33} + \dfrac{17}{33} = 1 + \dfrac{17 \times 3}{33 \times 3} = 1 + \dfrac{51}{99} = 1 + 0.\overline{51} = 1.\overline{51}$

4) $\dfrac{85}{9} = \dfrac{81+4}{9} = \dfrac{81}{9} + \dfrac{4}{9} = 9 + \dfrac{4}{9} = 9 + 0.\overline{4} = 9.\overline{4}$

5) $\dfrac{1}{12} = \dfrac{1 \times 75}{12 \times 75} = \dfrac{75}{900} = \dfrac{1}{100} \times \dfrac{75}{9} = \dfrac{1}{100} \times \left(\dfrac{72+3}{9}\right) = \dfrac{1}{100} \times \left(\dfrac{72}{9} + \dfrac{3}{9}\right)$
$= \dfrac{1}{100} \times \left(8 + \dfrac{3}{9}\right) = \dfrac{1}{100} \times (8 + 0.\overline{3}) = \dfrac{1}{100} \times 8.\overline{3} = 0.08\overline{3}$ (only the 3 is under the bar)

Answer Key

6) $\frac{25}{11} = \frac{22+3}{11} = \frac{22}{11} + \frac{3}{11} = 2 + \frac{3}{11} = 2 + \frac{3 \times 9}{11 \times 9} = 2 + \frac{27}{99} = 2 + 0.\overline{27} = 2.\overline{27}$

7) $\frac{11}{30} = \frac{11 \times 3}{30 \times 3} = \frac{33}{90} = \frac{1}{10} \times \frac{33}{9} = \frac{1}{10} \times \left(\frac{27+6}{9}\right) = \frac{1}{10} \times \left(\frac{27}{9} + \frac{6}{9}\right)$

$= \frac{1}{10} \times \left(3 + \frac{6}{9}\right) = \frac{1}{10} \times (3 + 0.\overline{6}) = \frac{1}{10} \times 3.\overline{6} = 0.3\overline{6}$ (only the 6 is under the bar)

8) $\frac{140}{111} = \frac{111+29}{111} = \frac{111}{111} + \frac{29}{111} = 1 + \frac{29}{111} = 1 + \frac{29 \times 9}{111 \times 9} = 1 + \frac{261}{999} = 1 + 0.\overline{261} = 1.\overline{261}$

9) $\frac{7}{22} = \frac{7 \times 45}{22 \times 45} = \frac{315}{990} = \frac{1}{10} \times \frac{315}{99} = \frac{1}{10} \times \left(\frac{297+18}{99}\right) = \frac{1}{10} \times \left(\frac{297}{99} + \frac{18}{99}\right)$

$= \frac{1}{10} \times \left(3 + \frac{18}{99}\right) = \frac{1}{10} \times (3 + 0.\overline{18}) = \frac{1}{10} \times 3.\overline{18} = 0.3\overline{18}$ (only the 18 is under the bar)

10) $\frac{2}{15} = \frac{2 \times 6}{15 \times 6} = \frac{12}{90} = \frac{1}{10} \times \frac{12}{9} = \frac{1}{10} \times \left(\frac{9+3}{9}\right) = \frac{1}{10} \times \left(\frac{9}{9} + \frac{3}{9}\right)$

$= \frac{1}{10} \times \left(1 + \frac{3}{9}\right) = \frac{1}{10} \times (1 + 0.\overline{3}) = \frac{1}{10} \times 1.\overline{3} = 0.1\overline{3}$ (only the 3 is under the bar)

11) $\frac{10}{3} = \frac{9+1}{3} = \frac{9}{3} + \frac{1}{3} = 3 + \frac{1}{3} = 3 + \frac{1 \times 3}{3 \times 3} = 3 + \frac{3}{9} = 3 + 0.\overline{3} = 3.\overline{3}$

12) $\frac{1}{36} = \frac{1 \times 25}{36 \times 25} = \frac{25}{900} = \frac{1}{100} \times \frac{25}{9} = \frac{1}{100} \times \left(\frac{18+7}{9}\right) = \frac{1}{100} \times \left(\frac{18}{9} + \frac{7}{9}\right)$

$= \frac{1}{100} \times \left(2 + \frac{7}{9}\right) = \frac{1}{100} \times (2 + 0.\overline{7}) = \frac{1}{100} \times 2.\overline{7} = 0.02\overline{7}$ (only the 7 is under the bar)

13) $\frac{7}{225} = \frac{7 \times 4}{225 \times 4} = \frac{28}{900} = \frac{1}{100} \times \frac{28}{9} = \frac{1}{100} \times \left(\frac{27+1}{9}\right) = \frac{1}{100} \times \left(\frac{27}{9} + \frac{1}{9}\right)$

$= \frac{1}{100} \times \left(3 + \frac{1}{9}\right) = \frac{1}{100} \times (3 + 0.\overline{1}) = \frac{1}{100} \times 3.\overline{1} = 0.03\overline{1}$ (only the 1 is under the bar)

14) $\frac{47}{15} = \frac{45+2}{15} = \frac{45}{15} + \frac{2}{15} = 3 + \frac{2}{15} = 3 + \frac{2 \times 6}{15 \times 6} = 3 + \frac{12}{90} = 3 + \frac{1}{10} \times \frac{12}{9}$

$= 3 + \frac{1}{10} \times \left(\frac{9+3}{9}\right) = 3 + \frac{1}{10} \times \left(\frac{9}{9} + \frac{3}{9}\right) = 3 + \frac{1}{10} \times \left(1 + \frac{3}{9}\right)$

$= 3 + \frac{1}{10} \times (1 + 0.\overline{3}) = 3 + \frac{1}{10} \times 1.\overline{3} = 3 + 0.1\overline{3} = 3.1\overline{3}$ (only the 3 is under the bar)

15) $\frac{1}{24} = \frac{1 \times 375}{24 \times 375} = \frac{375}{9000} = \frac{1}{1000} \times \frac{375}{9} = \frac{1}{1000} \times \left(\frac{369+6}{9}\right) = \frac{1}{1000} \times \left(\frac{369}{9} + \frac{6}{9}\right)$

$= \frac{1}{1000} \times \left(41 + \frac{6}{9}\right) = \frac{1}{1000} \times (41 + 0.\overline{6}) = \frac{1}{1000} \times 41.\overline{6} = 0.041\overline{6}$ (only the 6 repeats)

16) $\frac{9}{55} = \frac{9 \times 18}{55 \times 18} = \frac{162}{990} = \frac{1}{10} \times \frac{162}{99} = \frac{1}{10} \times \left(\frac{99+63}{99}\right) = \frac{1}{10} \times \left(\frac{99}{99} + \frac{63}{99}\right)$

$= \frac{1}{10} \times \left(1 + \frac{63}{99}\right) = \frac{1}{10} \times (1 + 0.\overline{63}) = \frac{1}{10} \times 1.\overline{63} = 0.1\overline{63}$ (only the 63 is under the bar)

17) $\frac{25}{6} = \frac{24+1}{6} = \frac{24}{6} + \frac{1}{6} = 4 + \frac{1}{6} = 4 + \frac{1 \times 15}{6 \times 15} = 4 + \frac{15}{90} = 4 + \frac{1}{10} \times \frac{15}{9}$

$= 4 + \frac{1}{10} \times \left(\frac{9+6}{9}\right) = 4 + \frac{1}{10} \times \left(\frac{9}{9} + \frac{6}{9}\right) = 4 + \frac{1}{10} \times \left(1 + \frac{6}{9}\right)$

$= 4 + \frac{1}{10} \times (1 + 0.\overline{6}) = 4 + \frac{1}{10} \times 1.\overline{6} = 4 + 0.1\overline{6} = 4.1\overline{6}$ (only the 6 is under the bar)

18) $\frac{8}{7} = \frac{7+1}{7} = \frac{7}{7} + \frac{1}{7} = 1 + \frac{1}{7} = 1 + \frac{1 \times 142{,}857}{7 \times 142{,}857} = 1 + \frac{142{,}857}{999{,}999} = 1 + 0.\overline{142857} = 1.\overline{142857}$

19) $\frac{3}{275} = \frac{3 \times 36}{275 \times 36} = \frac{108}{9900} = \frac{1}{100} \times \frac{108}{99} = \frac{1}{100} \times \left(\frac{99+9}{99}\right) = \frac{1}{100} \times \left(\frac{99}{99} + \frac{9}{99}\right)$

$= \frac{1}{100} \times \left(1 + \frac{9}{99}\right) = \frac{1}{100} \times (1 + 0.\overline{09}) = \frac{1}{100} \times 1.\overline{09} = 0.01\overline{09}$ (only the 09 repeats)

20) $\frac{1}{75} = \frac{1 \times 12}{75 \times 12} = \frac{12}{900} = \frac{1}{100} \times \frac{12}{9} = \frac{1}{100} \times \left(\frac{9+3}{9}\right) = \frac{1}{100} \times \left(\frac{9}{9} + \frac{3}{9}\right)$

$= \frac{1}{100} \times \left(1 + \frac{3}{9}\right) = \frac{1}{100} \times (1 + 0.\overline{3}) = \frac{1}{100} \times 1.\overline{3} = 0.01\overline{3}$ (only the 3 is under the bar)

Exercise Set 7.7

1) $2.\overline{63} = 2 + 0.\overline{63} = 2 + \frac{63}{99} = 2 + \frac{63 \div 9}{99 \div 9} = 2 + \frac{7}{11} = \boxed{2\frac{7}{11}}$ or $\frac{2 \times 11 + 7}{11} = \frac{22+7}{11} = \boxed{\frac{29}{11}}$

2) $0.\overline{56} = \boxed{\frac{56}{99}}$

3) $0.5\overline{6} = 0.5 + 0.0\overline{6} = \frac{5}{10} + \frac{1}{10} \times 0.\overline{6} = \frac{5}{10} + \frac{1}{10} \times \frac{6}{9}$

$= \frac{5}{10} + \frac{6}{90} = \frac{5 \times 9}{10 \times 9} + \frac{6}{90} = \frac{45}{90} + \frac{6}{90} = \frac{51}{90} = \frac{51 \div 3}{90 \div 3} = \boxed{\frac{17}{30}}$

4) $0.0\overline{48} = \frac{1}{10} \times 0.\overline{48} = \frac{1}{10} \times \frac{48}{99} = \frac{48}{990} = \frac{48 \div 6}{990 \div 6} = \boxed{\frac{8}{165}}$

5) $0.04\overline{8} = 0.04 + 0.00\overline{8} = \frac{4}{100} + \frac{1}{100} \times 0.\overline{8} = \frac{4}{100} + \frac{1}{100} \times \frac{8}{9}$

$= \frac{4}{100} + \frac{8}{900} = \frac{4 \times 9}{100 \times 9} + \frac{8}{900} = \frac{36}{900} + \frac{8}{900} = \frac{44}{900} = \frac{44 \div 4}{900 \div 4} = \boxed{\frac{11}{225}}$

6) $0.\overline{048} = \frac{048}{999} = \frac{48}{999} = \frac{48 \div 3}{999 \div 3} = \boxed{\frac{16}{333}}$

7) $1.0\overline{7} = 1 + 0.0\overline{7} = 1 + \frac{1}{10} \times 0.\overline{7} = 1 + \frac{1}{10} \times \frac{7}{9} = 1 + \frac{7}{90} = \boxed{1\frac{7}{90}}$ or $\frac{1 \times 90 + 7}{90} = \boxed{\frac{97}{90}}$

8) $0.00\overline{96} = \frac{1}{100} \times 0.\overline{96} = \frac{1}{100} \times \frac{96}{99} = \frac{96}{9900} = \frac{96 \div 12}{9900 \div 12} = \boxed{\frac{8}{825}}$

9) $0.\overline{612} = \frac{612}{999} = \frac{612 \div 9}{999 \div 9} = \boxed{\frac{68}{111}}$

10) $2.\overline{50} = 2 + 0.\overline{50} = 2 + \frac{50}{99} = \boxed{2\frac{50}{99}}$ or $\frac{2 \times 99 + 50}{99} = \boxed{\frac{248}{99}}$

Note: $2.\overline{50}$ means 2.50505050... (It does **not** mean 2.5, which is $\frac{5}{2}$.)

11) $0.000\overline{72} = \frac{1}{1000} \times 0.\overline{72} = \frac{1}{1000} \times \frac{72}{99} = \frac{72}{99{,}000} = \frac{72 \div 72}{99{,}000 \div 72} = \boxed{\frac{1}{1375}}$

Answer Key

12) $0.03\overline{8} = 0.03 + 0.00\overline{8} = \frac{3}{100} + \frac{1}{100} \times 0.\overline{8} = \frac{3}{100} + \frac{1}{100} \times \frac{8}{9}$

$= \frac{3}{100} + \frac{8}{900} = \frac{3 \times 9}{100 \times 9} + \frac{8}{900} = \frac{27}{900} + \frac{8}{900} = \frac{35}{900} = \frac{35 \div 5}{900 \div 5} = \boxed{\frac{7}{180}}$

13) $4.\overline{225} = 4 + 0.\overline{225} = 4 + \frac{225}{999} = 4 + \frac{225 \div 9}{999 \div 9} = 4 + \frac{25}{111} = \boxed{4\frac{25}{111}}$ or $\frac{4 \times 111 + 25}{111} = \boxed{\frac{469}{111}}$

14) $0.36\overline{1} = 0.36 + 0.00\overline{1} = \frac{36}{100} + \frac{1}{100} \times 0.\overline{1} = \frac{36}{100} + \frac{1}{100} \times \frac{1}{9}$

$= \frac{36}{100} + \frac{1}{900} = \frac{36 \times 9}{100 \times 9} + \frac{1}{900} = \frac{324}{900} + \frac{1}{900} = \frac{325}{900} = \frac{325 \div 25}{900 \div 25} = \boxed{\frac{13}{36}}$

15) $1.\overline{45} = 1 + 0.\overline{45} = 1 + \frac{45}{99} = 1 + \frac{45 \div 9}{99 \div 9} = 1 + \frac{5}{11} = \boxed{1\frac{5}{11}}$ or $\frac{1 \times 11 + 5}{11} = \boxed{\frac{16}{11}}$

16) $0.009\overline{3} = 0.009 + 0.000\overline{3} = \frac{9}{1000} + \frac{1}{1000} \times 0.\overline{3} = \frac{9}{1000} + \frac{1}{1000} \times \frac{3}{9}$

$= \frac{9}{1000} + \frac{3}{9000} = \frac{9 \times 9}{1000 \times 9} + \frac{3}{9000} = \frac{81}{9000} + \frac{3}{9000} = \frac{84}{9000} = \frac{84 \div 12}{9000 \div 12} = \boxed{\frac{7}{750}}$

17) $0.11\overline{36} = 0.11 + 0.00\overline{36} = \frac{11}{100} + \frac{1}{100} \times 0.\overline{36} = \frac{11}{100} + \frac{1}{100} \times \frac{36}{99}$

$= \frac{11}{100} + \frac{36}{9900} = \frac{11 \times 11}{100 \times 11} + \frac{36 \div 9}{9900 \div 9} = \frac{121}{1100} + \frac{4}{1100} = \frac{125}{1100} = \frac{125 \div 25}{1100 \div 25} = \boxed{\frac{5}{44}}$

18) $1.291\overline{6} = 1.291 + 0.000\overline{6} = \frac{1291}{1000} + \frac{1}{1000} \times 0.\overline{6} = \frac{1291}{1000} + \frac{1}{1000} \times \frac{6}{9}$

$= \frac{1291}{1000} + \frac{6}{9000} = \frac{1291 \times 9}{1000 \times 9} + \frac{6}{9000} = \frac{11{,}619}{9000} + \frac{6}{9000} = \frac{11{,}625}{9000} = \frac{11{,}625 \div 375}{9000 \div 375} = \boxed{\frac{31}{24}}$ or $\boxed{1\frac{7}{24}}$

19) $0.21\overline{3} = 0.21 + 0.00\overline{3} = \frac{21}{100} + \frac{1}{100} \times 0.\overline{3} = \frac{21}{100} + \frac{1}{100} \times \frac{3}{9}$

$= \frac{21}{100} + \frac{3}{900} = \frac{21 \times 9}{100 \times 9} + \frac{3}{900} = \frac{189}{900} + \frac{3}{900} = \frac{192}{900} = \frac{192 \div 12}{900 \div 12} = \boxed{\frac{16}{75}}$

20) $0.\overline{761904} = \frac{761{,}904 \div 47{,}619}{999{,}999 \div 47{,}619} = \boxed{\frac{16}{21}}$ Note: It is okay to do this in several steps. It will help if you are familiar with divisibility tests (such as how to tell whether or not a whole number is evenly divisible by 4 or 9).

Chapter 8 Percents and Decimals

Exercise Set 8.1

1) $25\% = 25 \div 100 = 0.25$
2) $0.6\% = 0.6 \div 100 = 0.006$
3) $3.79\% = 3.79 \div 100 = 0.0379$
4) $130\% = 130 \div 100 = 1.30 = 1.3$
5) $80\% = 80 \div 100 = 0.80 = 0.8$
6) $0.04\% = 0.04 \div 100 = 0.0004$
7) $0.865\% = 0.865 \div 100 = 0.00865$
8) $16.3\% = 16.3 \div 100 = 0.163$
9) $400\% = 400 \div 100 = 4$
10) $6.2\% = 6.2 \div 100 = 0.062$
11) $0.028\% = 0.028 \div 100 = 0.00028$
12) $0.1257\% = 0.1257 \div 100 = 0.001257$
13) $57.36\% = 57.36 \div 100 = 0.5736$
14) $0.009\% = 0.009 \div 100 = 0.00009$
15) $0.34\% = 0.34 \div 100 = 0.0034$
16) $216\% = 216 \div 100 = 2.16$
17) $156.27\% = 156.27 \div 100 = 1.5627$
18) $0.0871\% = 0.0871 \div 100 = 0.000871$
19) $2.626\% = 2.626 \div 100 = 0.02626$
20) $0.0001\% = 0.0001 \div 100 = 0.000001$

Exercise Set 8.2

1) $1.2 = 1.2 \times 100\% = 120\%$
2) $0.091 = 0.091 \times 100\% = 9.1\%$
3) $0.8 = 0.8 \times 100\% = 80\%$
4) $0.0001 = 0.0001 \times 100\% = 0.01\%$
5) $0.007 = 0.007 \times 100\% = 0.7\%$
6) $8.842 = 8.842 \times 100\% = 884.2\%$
7) $0.364 = 0.364 \times 100\% = 36.4\%$
8) $0.0025 = 0.0025 \times 100\% = 0.25\%$
9) $4 = 4 \times 100\% = 400\%$
10) $0.109 = 0.109 \times 100\% = 10.9\%$
11) $0.0563 = 0.0563 \times 100\% = 5.63\%$
12) $0.00006 = 0.00006 \times 100\% = 0.006\%$
13) $0.00979 = 0.00979 \times 100\% = 0.979\%$
14) $0.45 = 0.45 \times 100\% = 45\%$

Exercise Set 8.3

1) $50\% \times 9 = 0.5 \times 9 = 4.5$
2) $4\% \times 8 = 0.04 \times 8 = 0.32$
3) $0.2\% \times 3 = 0.002 \times 3 = 0.006$
4) $300\% \times 6 = 3 \times 6 = 18$
5) $75\% \times 4 = 0.75 \times 4 = 3.00 = 3$
6) $8\% \times 12 = 0.08 \times 12 = 0.96$
7) $0.63\% \times 4 = 0.0063 \times 4 = 0.0252$
8) $0.025\% \times 7 = 0.00025 \times 7 = 0.00175$

Note: You should perform the multiplication like we did in Chapter 4.

9) $5.4\% \times 9 = 0.054 \times 9 = 0.486$
10) $0.3\% \times 22 = 0.003 \times 22 = 0.066$

Answer Key

11) $48\% \times 16 = 0.48 \times 16 = 7.68$ 12) $3.7\% \times 6.1 = 0.037 \times 6.1 = 0.2257$

Note: You should perform the multiplication like we did in Chapter 4.

13) $120\% \times 87 = 1.2 \times 87 = 104.4$ 14) $0.68\% \times 9.2 = 0.0068 \times 9.2 = 0.06256$

15) $4.9\% \times 0.55 = 0.049 \times 0.55 = 0.02695$ 16) $74\% \times 239 = 0.74 \times 239 = 176.86$

Exercise Set 8.4

1) $60 \times 0.15 = 9$ such that $60 + 9 = \boxed{69}$

Note: You should perform the arithmetic like we have in previous chapters, meaning that you should show more work than we have shown here.

2) $12 \times 0.7 = 8.4$ such that $12 - 8.4 = \boxed{3.6}$

3) $\frac{45-36}{36} = \frac{9}{36} = 9 \div 36 = 0.25 = 25\%$ This is a $\boxed{25\%}$ increase.

4) $\frac{7.2-1.8}{7.2} = \frac{5.4}{7.2} = 5.4 \div 7.2 = 0.75 = 75\%$ This is a $\boxed{75\%}$ decrease.

5) $4.2 \times 0.05 = 0.21$ such that $4.2 - 0.21 = \boxed{3.99}$

6) $\frac{474-316}{316} = \frac{158}{316} = 158 \div 316 = 0.5 = 50\%$ This is a $\boxed{50\%}$ increase.

7) $0.85 \times 0.6 = 0.51$ such that $0.85 + 0.51 = \boxed{1.36}$

8) $\frac{0.068-0.0442}{0.068} = \frac{0.0238}{0.068} = 0.0238 \div 0.068 = 0.35 = 35\%$ This is a $\boxed{35\%}$ decrease.

Exercise Set 8.5

1) tax $= \$3.60 \times 0.075 = \$0.27$; total cost $= \$3.60 + \$0.27 = \boxed{\$3.87}$

Note: You should perform the arithmetic like we have in previous chapters, meaning that you should show more work than we have shown here.

2) discount $= \$795 \times 0.15 = \$119.25$; total cost $= \$795 - \$119.25 = \boxed{\$675.75}$

3) discount $= \$140 \times 0.3 = \$42$; subtotal $= \$140 - \$42 = \$98$

tax $= \$98 \times 0.1 = \$9.8$; total cost $= \$98 + \$9.8 = \boxed{\$107.80}$

Note: It is incorrect to subtract 10% from 30% to get 20% and apply 20% to $140. Why? Because 30% is applied to the price tag of $140, whereas 10% is applied to the subtotal of $98. Since the two percents apply to **different** amounts, they can not be combined by subtracting them.

4) $15 \div 20 = 0.75 = \boxed{75\%}$

5) amount of change $= 25 \times 0.16 = 4$; final amount $= 25 - 4 = \boxed{21}$

Exercise Set 8.6

1) $0.032 < 4.9\%$ (since $4.9\% = 0.049$)

2) $\frac{3}{4} < 80\%$ (since $\frac{3}{4} = 0.75$ and $80\% = 0.8$)

Note: You should show more work for $\frac{3}{4} = 0.75$ (like we did in Chapter 6).

3) $\frac{8}{5} > 150\%$ (since $\frac{8}{5} = 1.6$ and $150\% = 1.5$)

4) $4.2 > 78\%$ (since $78\% = 0.78$)

5) $0.3\% < 0.02$ (since $0.3\% = 0.003$)

6) $\frac{2}{3} < 70\%$ (since $\frac{2}{3} = 0.\overline{6}$ and $70\% = 0.7$)

Note: You should show more work for $\frac{2}{3} = 0.\overline{6}$ (like we did in Chapter 7).

7) $325\% < \frac{7}{2}$ (since $325\% = 3.25$ and $\frac{7}{2} = 3.5$)

8) $64\% > 0.6$ (since $64\% = 0.64$)

9) $240\% < 3.1$ (since $240\% = 2.4$)

10) $63\% > \frac{5}{8}$ (since $63\% = 0.63$ and $\frac{5}{8} = 0.625$)

11) $0.037 > 0.51\%$ (since $0.51\% = 0.0051$)

12) $\frac{8}{11} > 72\%$ (since $\frac{8}{11} = 0.\overline{72}$ and $72\% = 0.72$)

Recall from Chapter 7 that $0.\overline{72}$ means $0.72727272...$

13) $\frac{9}{20} = 45\%$ (since $\frac{9}{20} = 0.45$ and $45\% = 0.45$)

14) $0.12 > 8.4\%$ (since $8.4\% = 0.084$)

15) $28\% > 0.02$ (since $28\% = 0.28$)

16) $116\% < \frac{7}{6}$ (since $116\% = 1.16$ and $\frac{7}{6} = 1.1\overline{6}$

Recall from Chapter 7 that $1.1\overline{6}$ means $1.166666666...$

Chapter 9 Estimate with Decimals

Exercise Set 9.1

1) 1.6_7_4 ≈ 1.7 (to the nearest tenth)
2) 0.58_3_9 ≈ 0.58 (to the nearest hundredth)
3) 42.4_8_ ≈ 42.5 (to the nearest tenth)
4) 0.05_4_ ≈ 0.05 (to the nearest hundredth)
5) 74._6_1 ≈ 75 (to the nearest unit)
6) 0.4_5_ ≈ 0.5 (to the nearest tenth)
7) 0.088_2_ ≈ 0.088 (to the nearest thousandth)
8) 0.10_8_ ≈ 0.11 (to the nearest hundredth)
9) 724._5_3 ≈ 725 (to the nearest unit)
10) 0.534_9_2 ≈ 0.535 (to the nearest thousandth)
11) 77.8_4_6 ≈ 77.8 (to the nearest tenth)
12) 2.93_5_7 ≈ 2.94 (to the nearest hundredth)
13) 86._4_68 ≈ 86 (to the nearest unit)
14) 0.001_9_1 ≈ 0.002 (to the nearest thousandth)
15) 7._5_ ≈ 8 (to the nearest unit)
16) 0.00_9_4 ≈ 0.01 (to the nearest hundredth)
17) 9.9_4_9 ≈ 9.9 (to the nearest tenth)
18) 0._6_321 ≈ 1 (to the nearest unit)
19) 0.454_5_4 ≈ 0.455 (to the nearest thousandth)
20) 0.0_8_4 ≈ 0.1 (to the nearest tenth)

Exercise Set 9.2

1) 0.9_5_ ≈ 1.0, which is equivalent to 1 (to the nearest tenth)
2) 2.99_9_ ≈ 3.00, which is equivalent to 3 (to the nearest hundredth)
3) 49._7_ ≈ 50 (to the nearest unit)
4) 0.19_8_ ≈ 0.20, which is equivalent to 0.2 (to the nearest hundredth)
5) 7.9_6_ ≈ 8.0, which is equivalent to 8 (to the nearest tenth)

6) $0.0059\underline{5} \approx 0.0060$, which is equivalent to 0.006 (to the nearest ten thousandth)
7) $119.99\underline{6}6 \approx 120.00$, which is equivalent to 120 (to the nearest hundredth)
8) $0.0899\underline{8} \approx 0.0900$, which is equivalent to 0.09 (to the nearest ten thousandth)
9) $0.099\underline{5}7 \approx 0.100$, which is equivalent to 0.1 (to the nearest thousandth)

Exercise Set 9.3

1) $0.82 + 0.67 \approx 0.8 + 0.7 = 1.5$ (to the nearest tenth)
Note: You may wish to stack the numbers vertically like we did in Chapter 3.
2) $6.27 + 1.74 \approx 6 + 2 = 8$ (to the nearest unit)
3) $0.7652 + 0.4348 \approx 0.77 + 0.43 = 1.20 = 1.2$ (to the nearest hundredth)
4) $6.83 + 4.18 \approx 6.8 + 4.2 = 11$ (to the nearest tenth)
5) $0.00876 + 0.006482 \approx 0.009 + 0.006 = 0.015$ (to the nearest thousandth)
6) $36.2 + 19.6 \approx 36 + 20 = 56$ (to the nearest unit)
7) $2.46 + 0.085 \approx 2.5 + 0.1 = 2.6$ (to the nearest tenth)
8) $0.49983 + 0.02971 \approx 0.500 + 0.030 = 0.530 = 0.53$ (to the nearest thousandth)
9) $0.098 + 0.0089 \approx 0.10 + 0.01 = 0.11$ (to the nearest hundredth)
10) $42.54 + 29.96 \approx 42.5 + 30.0 = 72.5$ (to the nearest tenth)

Exercise Set 9.4

1) $12.17 - 4.83 \approx 12.2 - 4.8 = 7.4$ (to the nearest tenth)
2) $1.437 - 0.5544 \approx 1.44 - 0.55 = 0.89$ (to the nearest hundredth)
3) $26.25 - 8.61 \approx 26 - 9 = 17$ (to the nearest unit)
4) $0.0632 - 0.00909 \approx 0.06 - 0.01 = 0.05$ (to the nearest hundredth)
5) $0.0077 - 0.0024 \approx 0.008 - 0.002 = 0.006$ (to the nearest thousandth)
6) $0.903 - 0.2814 \approx 0.9 - 0.3 = 0.6$ (to the nearest tenth)
7) $0.746 - 0.381 \approx 0.75 - 0.38 = 0.37$ (to the nearest hundredth)
8) $19.62 - 7.58 \approx 20 - 8 = 12$ (to the nearest unit)
9) $0.997 - 0.599 \approx 1.00 - 0.60 = 0.40 = 0.4$ (to the nearest hundredth)
10) $0.238 - 0.0755 \approx 0.238 - 0.076 = 0.162$ (to the nearest thousandth)

Answer Key

Exercise Set 9.5

1) $7.89 \times 3.12 \approx 8 \times 3 = 24$ 2) $6.42 \times 0.571 \approx 6 \times 0.6 = 3.6$
3) $0.914 \times 0.809 \approx 0.9 \times 0.8 = 0.72$ 4) $28.4 \times 3.9 \approx 30 \times 4 = 120$

Note: If you keep more digits, your answer will be more precise.

5) $0.0441 \times 0.0763 \approx 0.04 \times 0.08 = 0.0032$ 6) $1.989 \times 0.39 \approx 2 \times 0.4 = 0.8$
7) $0.28 \times 0.041 \approx 0.3 \times 0.04 = 0.012$ 8) $0.055 \times 0.00147 \approx 0.06 \times 0.001 = 0.00006$

Note: In Exercise 8, rounding 0.00147 down to 0.001 results in a significant error (as the exact answer is 0.00008085). You can get a better answer by rounding 0.00147 to two significant figures instead of one (but rounding 0.00147 to 0.001 is satisfactory for the purpose of the exercises in this chapter).

9) $7.07 \times 0.0049 \approx 7 \times 0.005 = 0.035$
10) $0.0038 \times 0.00021 \approx 0.004 \times 0.0002 = 0.0000008$

Exercise Set 9.6

1) $2.69 \div 0.318 \approx 2.7 \div 0.3 = 9$ 2) $0.147 \div 0.308 \approx 0.15 \div 0.3 = 0.5$
3) $2.82 \div 0.069 \approx 2.8 \div 0.07 = 40$ 4) $0.043 \div 0.689 \approx 0.042 \div 0.7 = 0.06$

Note: We are not rounding each number. Rather, we are looking for a division fact that is a close approximation. We changed 0.043 to 0.042 because $0.042 \div 0.7 = 0.06$ is a division fact that is close to $0.043 \div 0.689$. The same idea applies to the other problems in this section.

5) $0.612 \div 0.0019 \approx 0.6 \div 0.002 = 300$ 6) $0.0338 \div 4.84 \approx 0.035 \div 5 = 0.007$
7) $1.598 \div 0.797 \approx 1.6 \div 0.8 = 2$ 8) $0.0063 \div 0.079 \approx 0.0064 \div 0.08 = 0.08$
9) $4.398 \div 0.00496 \approx 4.5 \div 0.005 = 900$
10) $0.00096 \div 9.984 \approx 0.0010 \div 10 = 0.0001$

WAS THIS BOOK HELPFUL?

A great deal of effort and thought was put into this book, such as:
- Breaking down the solutions to help make the math easier to understand.
- Careful selection of examples and problems for their instructional value.
- Full solutions to the exercises included in the answer key.

If you appreciate the effort that went into making this book possible, there is a simple way that you could show it:

<u>Please take a moment to post an honest review.</u>

For example, you can review this book at Amazon.com or Goodreads.com.

Even a short review can be helpful and will be much appreciated. If you're not sure what to write, following are a few ideas, though it's best to describe what is important to you.
- How much did you learn from reading and using this workbook?
- Were the solutions at the back of the book helpful?
- Were you able to understand the solutions?
- Was it helpful to follow the examples while solving the problems?
- Would you recommend this book to others? If so, why?

Do you believe that you found a mistake? Please email the author, Chris McMullen, at greekphysics@yahoo.com to ask about it. One of two things will happen:
- You might discover that it wasn't a mistake after all and learn why.
- You might be right, in which case the author will be grateful and future readers will benefit from the correction. Everyone is human.

ABOUT THE AUTHOR

Dr. Chris McMullen has over 20 years of experience teaching university physics in California, Oklahoma, Pennsylvania, and Louisiana. Dr. McMullen is also an author of math and science workbooks. Whether in the classroom or as a writer, Dr. McMullen loves sharing knowledge and the art of motivating and engaging students.

The author earned his Ph.D. in phenomenological high-energy physics (particle physics) from Oklahoma State University in 2002. Originally from California, Chris McMullen earned his Master's degree from California State University, Northridge, where his thesis was in the field of electron spin resonance.

As a physics teacher, Dr. McMullen observed that many students lack fluency in fundamental math skills. In an effort to help students of all ages and levels master essential math skills, he published a series of math workbooks on arithmetic, fractions, long division, word problems, prealgebra, algebra, geometry, trigonometry, logarithms, and calculus entitled *Improve Your Math Fluency*. Dr. McMullen has also published a variety of science books, including astronomy, chemistry, and physics workbooks.

Author, Chris McMullen, Ph.D.

PUZZLES

The author of this book, Chris McMullen, enjoys solving puzzles. His favorite puzzle is Kakuro (kind of like a cross between crossword puzzles and Sudoku). He once taught a three-week summer course on puzzles. If you enjoy mathematical pattern puzzles, you might appreciate:

300+ Mathematical Pattern Puzzles

Number Pattern Recognition & Reasoning
- Pattern recognition
- Visual discrimination
- Analytical skills
- Logic and reasoning
- Analogies
- Mathematics

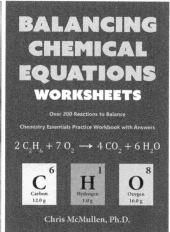

ARITHMETIC

For students who could benefit from additional arithmetic practice:
- Addition, subtraction, multiplication, and division facts
- Multi-digit addition and subtraction
- Addition and subtraction applied to clocks
- Multiplication with 10-20
- Multi-digit multiplication
- Long division with remainders
- Fractions
- Mixed fractions
- Decimals
- Fractions, decimals, and percentages
- Grade 5 and 6 math workbooks

www.improveyourmathfluency.com

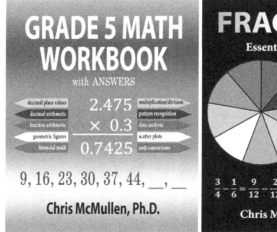
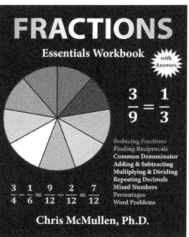

MATH

This series of math workbooks is geared toward practicing essential math skills:
- Prealgebra
- Algebra
- Geometry
- Trigonometry
- Logarithms
- Calculus
- Fractions, decimals, and percentages
- Long division
- Multiplication and division
- Addition and subtraction
- Roman numerals

www.improveyourmathfluency.com

SCIENCE

Dr. McMullen has published a variety of **science** books, including:
- Basic astronomy concepts
- Basic chemistry concepts
- Balancing chemical reactions
- Calculus-based physics textbooks
- Calculus-based physics workbooks
- Calculus-based physics examples
- Trig-based physics workbooks
- Trig-based physics examples
- Creative physics problems
- Modern physics

www.monkeyphysicsblog.wordpress.com

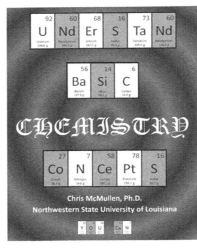
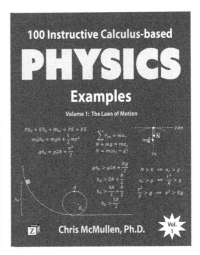

Made in the USA
Middletown, DE
21 September 2023